ONLY ONE WAY

Cleave To Jesus Christ

MARIA JOY

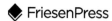 FriesenPress

Suite 300 - 990 Fort St
Victoria, BC, V8V 3K2
Canada

www.friesenpress.com

The Nelson Study Bible
Patsy Cline, She's Got You
Third Day, Soul On Fire

ISBN
978-1-5255-2009-9 (Hardcover)
978-1-5255-2010-5 (Paperback)
978-1-5255-2011-2 (eBook)

1. Biography & Autobiography, Personal Memoirs

Distributed to the trade by The Ingram Book Company

ONLY

ONE

WAY

"SIT DOWN OVER THERE, AND CLOSE YOUR EYES," the voice sneered, intimidating his hostage. I am hesitant. I feel shaky and uncertain, cautiously I take one step forward. A heavy iron door slammed shut behind me. I'm trapped inside the burrow and dead in my trespasses. I choke from smoky fumes lingering in the air. I'm sitting in darkness, cast in shadows of death. I was a tortured soul filled with fears that had me bolting down the stairs; there were so many twists and turns. My drug addiction to crystal meth led me here.

The night sends out it's chilling invitation. Tingling sensations run down the back of my neck. I'm spooked. I hear him whisper, *"Let me twist you from within."* And somehow, I feel him from within. I don't understand. His chair seems to move with my mind, and I never noticed. Woe. I'm bound in heavy irons.

Nothing is right in this room. His gravity begins turning the room upside down on its axis. I catch my silhouette splitting in two out of the corner of my eye. What remains of me is a stranger who I don't even know. I start to panic. I can't breathe, smothered in fatal desperation. What does he want from me? Currents of hostile rage shoot through my veins. I have turned into a wild injured animal, backed into the corner. I am powerless against this beast who is my tempter.

I thrash around hissing, trying to escape. "I'm no one's prisoner!" No matter how hard I try, I can't break free, which only fuels the animosity that rages within me. Like a lion on the prowl, he towers over me. His chest is so heavy. It is puffed out and it heaves as he breathes, up and down. Under his mask I sense how ancient and primal he is. I am terrified. There is no way to escape the loathing I see when I look into his eyes. He wants to devour me, like he wants to rip me into shreds.

"Now, now." the wicked one jeers. *"I'm taking you to someplace special."* And he covered my eyes.

When the blindfold is off, I'm still blind.

I look up. Vultures circle up in the sky.

I'm sinking in a pit of deep mire and cannot move.

My depth of sanity was lost long ago. It's not just me; they sense it too.

I'm lost in my own retribution.

"Keep digging!" The Joker hands me a shovel, but I can't see.

"Where are we?" I ask hysterically, looking around, covered in filth.

"Just dig! Give me that! Here, I will dig for you!" commanded tyranny's exhausting voice. With unreachable reason, it left behind a shattered soul.

Where had everyone gone? My eyelids are heavy, shackled to chains weighed down into the depths of blackness. I can't keep my eyes from closing. I am seized to a lost world that pulled me under with it. All I know is this world does not belong to me. Crying and lost. *Man, these trenches are deep.* All along, I was digging a hole inside myself. I never realized; I am already dead.

Surely there must be a way out? Surely there must be hope?

Desperate for help, I heard my dad's voice. The sound travelled with the light, timeless in it's grace. The memory was from my childhood and I am startled from the impact. It was a mystery how the Word could find me. For it was still buried deep in a place of understanding.

> *"Blessed is the man who walks not in the counsel of the ungodly, nor stands in the path of sinners, nor sits in the seat of the scornful; but his delight is in the law of the Lord, and in His law, he meditates day and night. He shall be like a tree planted by the rivers of water that brings forth its fruit in its season, whose leaf also shall not wither; and whatever he does shall prosper.*

The ungodly are not so, but are like the chaff which the wind drives away."

I am overwhelmed, with an intense longing to get back to the protection of the King. His name is Jesus Christ. His countenance surpasses the radiance of light. He possesses kindness that is *so* tender, and His greatest desire is to save a lost soul. It is written: "You were sold for nothing, and without money you will be redeemed. If you seek me, you will find me. Read my word, and I will unlock the mystery of God's grace through Jesus Christ. It is full of treasures that you put inside your chest. For the greatest riches of all, gives life to your soul."

Dearest Reader:

It is my privilege to share my on-going journey. Thank you for your kindness. In a world of blurred lines, I will make it crystal clear. For years I was one with the darkness. And now, I am persuaded that neither death nor life shall be able to separate us from the love of God that is in Christ Jesus.

I am excited to announce: freedom is happening through the power of the Holy Spirit.

With love,
Maria Joy

For I, the Lord your God, will hold your right hand,
saying to you, 'Fear not, I will help you.' Isaiah 41:13

I will extol You, my God, O King; And I will bless Your name
forever and ever. Great is the Lord, and greatly to be praised; and
His greatness is unsearchable. One generation shall praise Your
works to another, and shall declare Your mighty acts. Psalms 145

For the word of God is living and powerful, and sharper
than any two-edged sword, piercing even to the division of
soul and spirit, and of joints and marrow, and is a discerner
of the thoughts and intents of the heart. Hebrews 4:12

What do you think? If a man owns a hundred sheep, and one of them
wanders away, will he not leave the ninety-nine on the hills and go to
look for the one that wandered off? And if he finds it, I tell you the
truth, he is happier about that one sheep than about the ninety-nine
that did not wander off. In the same way your Father in heaven is not
willing that any of these little ones should be lost. Matthew 18:12-14

Lest they see with their eyes, and hear with their
ears, and understand with their heart,

and return and be healed. Isaiah 6:10

Today, if you will hear His voice, do not
harden your hearts. Hebrews 4:7

For we do not wrestle against flesh and blood, but against principalities, against powers, against the rulers of the darkness of this age, against the spiritual hosts of wickedness in the heavenly places.

Ephesians 6:11-12

The Lord of hosts, Him you shall hallow; let Him be your fear, and let Him be your dread. Isaiah 8:13

He will separate them from one another, as a shepherd divides his sheep from the goats. And He will set His sheep on the right hand, but the goats on His left. Then the King will say to those on His right hand, "Come, you blessed of My Father, inherit the kingdom prepared for you from the foundation of the world." Then He will also say to those on the left hand, "Depart from Me, you cursed, into everlasting fire prepared for the devil and his angels." Then He answered them, saying, "Assuredly, I say to you, in as much as you did not do it to one of the least of these, you did not do it to Me." Matthew 25

ACKNOWLEDGEMENTS

The Highest God, My Lord Saviour Jesus Christ,
and the Holy Spirit; I exalt You.

Wisdom, Understanding, Revelation, and Knowledge; I extol You.

To my family. You helped pick up the pieces so many times.

Rita, Elvin, Theresa. Church family, and all
those who helped me over the years.

TABLE OF CONTENTS

PREFACE

In one exact moment, my life drastically shifted course. My world was silenced. I had experienced the tremendous power of answered prayer. I knew things would never be the same for me.

My cup overflows. I want it to spill over into other cups, trusting that it will impact other lives. May we keep finding and filling cups.

ONE
MISS TINKER BELL

I had been broken and rejected, and now, I'm the luckiest girl. I am a slow learner with a simple mind, but thankfully we are all given a patient teacher. All I have is because of God's mercy in my life. I'm righteously blessed and praying daily to be restored. I have felt the heavenly scales of justice tip, and the balance is now in my favour. The levy broke, and a wave of peace washed over me. It is incredible. I am learning that you have to "cleave to Jesus Christ" with everything that you have. It was *hard* testing of my faith to get my spiritual life back on the right track. I have seen the light, I know the way, and I am charged with one cause; "Follow Me." I'm Maria Joy, and my identity is found in Jesus Christ. Living within me is the Holy Spirit, it is an *unstoppable* force.

The world is completely different from the one I left all those years ago. Yes, sin once took me captive, but to my horror, it also took the world I once knew as well. The standards have slipped under the tapestries of evil. These so-called "freedoms" break into our minds and fear takes us hostage.

Life was simpler when I was a child because things looked more black or white. I was the baby with sun-blonde hair and blue-green eyes, who noticed the charm of others. I often tried to figure out who people were on the inside, but I was easily misled. I had to learn to turn and look up, and ask, "What is behind there?" Whether it floated or flew, it remained out of my grasp. I might be able to see it, but I could never hold it. Things tended to change like the day, except family, at least that is what I once thought. No, nothing is mine to keep. I appreciated simple things, like warm smiles and genuine kindness when you're feeling a bit down. Deep down, I thought the essence of life was found in the truth; the one thing that explains all. The wonders of the world cannot compete with what I have come to behold.

Through life's storms stood my dad. His faith never wavered. He came qualified, pure, and true, like his word. After a hard day's work, he would come home and give my mom a kiss. Dad would smile, telling us his own jokes that I didn't get. But that was okay. I still laughed because he laughed so hard after telling them – that was funny.

Mother had a hold of my heartstrings, tied to bind. I felt them so present. I could only go so far from her without feeling the natural pull back to her. I was a willing mamma's girl; my heart could not grapple with the idea of being apart from her for too long. No, nothing in life could drive us apart; anything that dare to try would be pure wicked indeed.

Remi was four years older then me. She was astute, stylish, the kind of person who would listen to others and give her best advice. I adored her as any little sister does. I sat on her bed every morning just to admire her. "You're so beautiful," I would tell her as she got ready for school. She had bright green eyes and took a lot of time curling her hair. At the time, she wore really big awkward-looking glasses.

"Really?" she replied. "Thanks." She smiled, looking back in the mirror. The memory is burned in my mind.

Both of my sisters were very attractive. Dallas was a year older than me. She had soft brown eyes that complimented her hair. Later on in life, she would keep the boys dangling on a string.

We lived on a picture-perfect farm near Nipawin, Saskatchewan. Dallas and I were walking out back and came up to an electric fence. Dallas looked around before spotting a long, broken branch lying nearby and picked it up. She was five years old and started giving me a quick tutorial. I was naive, but never convinced.

"Dallas, are you sure about this?" I questioned, standing in my black rubber boots.

She looked at me then back at the fence. "Yes, I saw Dad do it before."

I hesitated, "Well, okay."

With the stick in her hand, she slowly touched the very tip to the electric fence. Nothing happened. So, she grabbed hold of the fence with her other hand and immediately dropped the stick. I was horrified from her screaming. I should have learned right there.

When I was four, I woke up from a good night's sleep and it was natural that I called for Mom. I went outside looking for her. Where could she be? I walked to the end of the driveway with my feet getting further than my thoughts. Should I turn left to my Aunt Jewel's or right to my grandparents'? I looked both ways before I gave up and stared at the sky. I started spinning around till I felt dizzy, then opened my eyes and gave into the decision of travelling that dusty gravel road.

My baby steps took me first past the cemetery, where the dead rest, buried deep under the dirt. I remained focused. Sharp rocks were poking my bare feet and I could not help but cry. In no time, I passed the neighbours, a church, another neighbour, and finally I could see my aunt's house. It felt like five miles, but it was more like one. I turned around when I heard a noise. It was a car speeding fast, barrelling towards me. I quickly jumped off the shoulder of the road, waiting for the driver to come to their senses. It was my mom, and she looked like a nervous wreck.

"Joy! What are you doing?"

I choked back my tears, "I was looking all over for you. You were not in the house."

"No, I was on the phone. Don't ever do this again!"

Mom picked me up and put me in the car. As I stared out the window, I was thinking about my journey and how the long walk was now a quick drive home.

We arrived home, and I felt safe and sound, tucked under a mother's loving wing. Her feathers were the golden dust kind, but my feathers were the flowing red ribbon kind. I loved track and field – even more than my birthday. All the schools in the district would gather for one massive event. Sure, I may have gotten a couple second-place ribbons, but the blue was a pretty colour too. I made it in the local newspaper because I did well. We clipped the article out and kept it in my scrap-book. I planned to be in the Olympics.

When I was not running, I was riding on my little mustard yellow tricycle. I drove through mud puddles, often getting stuck. I faithfully greased it with the little red oil can, and the scent reminded me of my dad. I enjoyed picking Mother sweet smelling flowers. Some were bright purple and others were a little softer in colour. One of my favourite places was sitting under the lilac bush and playing with my little kitten Tinker Bell.

Our living room had high, vaulted ceilings and a feeling of coziness. Like flour carefully sifted, my parents were protective of what I saw on TV. I remember being six years old and watching Billy Graham preaching. A song started playing, "Come...just as you are..." I felt a calm, gentle, loving spirit speaking to my heart, so I needed to ask Mom what was going on.

"Mom, can you come in here, please?"

"What is it Joy?" She came and sat down on the rocking chair, picked me up, and put me on her lap.

"Well, what is this guy talking about? Why are all those people going up?"

I was that age where I had questions about everything.

"The verse John 3:16 says, "Jesus loved us so much that He died for our sins." Those people are asking Jesus into their hearts to be their Saviour and are given eternal life."

"Eternal life? Can I be saved too?" I asked hopeful.

"Yes, just pray after me." I bowed my head, folded my hands together, and prayed. I asked Jesus into my heart. Tears were softly rolling down my cheeks. It was a special feeling. I felt faith for the first time and a trust I knew was true. Smiling inside, the moment remained, a guarantee for this lifetime plus the next.

The seed of life was planted right there and then. Roots began to sprout around my heart and soul that only became stronger the more they were nurtured. I did not know much about gardening as a child. My parents would till the soil, dig holes, put a seed in the dirt, and cover it back up. Then, inch by inch, row by row, a garden grows. If you're lucky, when you're older, you grow strong into a mature fruit tree that stands by still waters, like my grandma. She delighted in Jesus. I just loved going over to her house for ice cream with sprinkles.

Grandma was 5'2", had light blue eyes, and short curly hair. She always wore two things: a smile and a dress. When I was there, she made a point to sing about Jesus, overflowing with bubbles of love. It had a huge impact on me. I wanted to be just like her when I grew up. If Jesus was her best friend, I wanted Him to be my best friend too. The one thing I asked to have from her when I was a bit older was her Bible. I knew it was her most precious treasure. To me, it felt like I would always have her if I had that special book.

My grandparents sent us to camp every summer. It had horses, archery, a swimming pool, crafts, and hayrides; plus, there was chapel a few times a day. At night, we sat around a campfire and sung along with the strumming of a guitar. I felt a "Presence," and my soul was surrendered to Jesus. These things I understood, and they were planted within the deepest part of me. When camp was over, my parents told us we were moving to Alberta. I was devastated. My perfect life was gone.

That night I could hear the tinkering of the rain falling down and I sat up on my bed. I looked above the transom of the window and saw lightning tantalizing my eyes and heard the thunder booming to get out. "Can I take you with me?" I asked the one who made the thunder. The breeze started rustling through the trees, stirring up dust. "If thou consider the dust, consider me also?" I waited for a response, and the rain started pouring down with my tears, celebrating their rights. Who can understand a sudden outburst of a child? Maybe the rain.

I was supposed to leave my entire identity behind. How was this even possible? I knew more who I was at that age than when I was older. What about the boy I had a crush on? I chased him at recess time, caught him, and threw him down hard on the ground. Once I had him pinned, he lay there helpless. We both giggled until I got off him. Sheldon was his name; he rode on my school bus. He had platinum blond hair. I planned to marry him when I was older. "No. I don't want to move."

The worst thing besides missing my grandparents was leaving my little tricycle behind with them. I had to accept the fact that the life I had built was gone, and no amount of tears would change anything.

I gazed up at the clouds, wishing I could use them as my pillow, then hopped back into bed and tucked myself under the linen sheets.

By the end of the summer, we were packed. With an eight-hour drive ahead of us and a moving van in tow, we headed for Drayton Valley, an oil town in Alberta. We were giving up a grand farm for a trailer on a lot.

It felt like a whole new world with lots to grip our curious imaginations. It was a fast pace in our new town, and one's income bracket dictated one's status. If you fell short, you were obligated to feel as though you did not quite measure up. Family came close second to making money. There wasn't much you could do but serve the meals and set the place cards. Company was invited over on Sundays and us children were sent away to play.

My dad was the one who disciplined us children. He was teaching us obedience, respect, and authority. My parents were over protective.

On Sunday, we piled in the car dressed in Sunday best. Our family found a church to attend, we were used to the small country church, and my parents decided on the Baptist church. Inside the carpet was green, and it matched the soft-seated bench pews. Jesus was the same, but the people were different. One Sunday in particular, the Holy Spirit caught my attention, and I listened closely. Pastor Bob had white hair and was warning the congregation sternly, "Never open your mind to the world, you have to protect it."

What did he mean? What was he talking about? Hmm. That was interesting. I carried the warning with me. I promised myself, "Okay, I will never open my mind."

It was definitely shaping up to look like this journey was going to be an uphill battle. It was as if we could hear a warning in the distance: "If you do what is right, will you not be accepted? But if you do not do what is right, sin is crouching at your door. It desires to have you, but you must master it."

Things like sin were not known to me. I adored the warmth of soft kittens, dressing them up and counting their stripes. I talked to them all day long, but people, on the other hand, were scary. Going into Grade 3, I had no friends in my new school, and I was incredibly shy. At first, I lucked out. I thought I had made myself a good friend, but by the next year, we were not friends anymore. She found a better friend who she liked playing with more than me, and I guess three's a crowd.

After school, I came home and told mom, "I have no friends." I would rather die than have to stand by dreadfully alone every day at recess time. I hoped the time would pass by quickly so that no one would see me standing by myself and feeling like a loser. Being an outsider made me wish I was invisible. Year after year, I took rejection to heart. Maybe I wore the wrong clothes. I definitely was not the smartest in math. These requirements challenged me, getting me down.

At night I called mom into my bedroom and asked the tough questions that waged war on my tender heart. "Why are kids so mean to me? Today, I was standing by the entrance, waiting for the bell to ring. This boy was there too and he called me a loser. Why does he pick on me?" I broke out in tears and started sobbing, as I felt the shame from earlier in the day. Mom was sad for me and gave me a hug.

"What was this boy's name?" she asked gently, moving the hair from out of my eyes.

I sniffled, "His name is Chase."

"That is not very nice. It is not true, Joy. You are very special. Jesus loves you so much."

Mom was incredibly gentle with my feelings.

"I would never be mean to anyone," I sobbed. I wanted so much to be liked.

"Tomorrow will be better. Let's pray about this right now, okay?"

"Okay."

Well, to me things were never okay. I was filled with fear every night at the thought of having to go to school the next day. At least I had one thing going for me – track and field. I looked forward to doing well in those competitions and trying to get a piece of myself back.

When track and field came around, I was pleased. I was wearing shorts and my hair was pulled back. This was my time to shine. I would get those other girls' attention and maybe make some friends. Maybe I would not feel so out of place here anymore. Maybe they would like me if I did really well.

My favourite event was coming up – running! We all lined up at the starting line, and I took off first when they said, "Go!" I was a fast starter and ran with all my might. Near the halfway mark, a girl started passing me, then another girl, and then another one. What was going on? This had never happened to me before. Any confidence I had those girls stole from me as they ran by. I didn't get last place, but I sure didn't get first. All the excitement over the hype of my most beloved day came crashing down. Every new event, I suddenly dreaded. I was devastated. Now the only thing I had to look forward to was the day being over and going for ice cream.

I was in Grade 5 when our family moved back out to a farm again. But oh, how I missed Tinker Bell, along with my grandparents. On this farm, my kittens were stolen by big ravens or hawks. Giant birds would come swooping down and scoop up my poor defenceless kittens right in front of me.

I was left with chores that I dreaded doing before school. I had to go inside the red chicken coop and feed those horrible, freaky looking hens. Sure, they were cute when they were soft little yellow chicks, but when they grew up, they walked funny, squawked, and pecked. We had over fifty of those buck-buck noisy things. They woke me up every morning. I was terrified to have to go and collect their eggs. They pecked at me. At each buck-buck, my anxiety worsened. The hens backed me into a corner, surrounded me. I had no way out. I had to defend myself against the mob. I kicked the stupid hens clear across the coop so they would back off. I launched them way up in the air, and they flew. Their wings spread out far. They glided through the air, and they squawked. My parents started discovering dead chickens in the coop and started talking about it at the table. "The chickens must be killing each other, pecking one another to death," my dad speculated. Whoops. I sat quietly, looking down at the table.

The trauma of raising chickens did not end there. We had to butcher them too. We woke up early at dawn. Each member of my family was assigned to a different station of the operation. My dad grabbed a hen and lay its poor head down on a wooden stump. He took an axe and chopped their heads off with one swift chop. These freaky chickens went crazy, running around with no head. Next, we dipped them in scolding hot water and plucked off all their feathers. It was a long day. We had to stick our hands up inside the chicken and de-gut them. It was disgusting to see their spleen, intestines, and guts spilling out. I became a vegetarian for years after the experience.

At the end of the day, we cleaned up and did something very nice for supper. It was my parents' way of showing their appreciation for all our hard work that day. Plus, we would usually make $60.

My family had lots of great times on the farm. Dad bought Dallas and I each our own horse. Dallas got a well trained, plain Quarter horse. I got the feisty fun one that loved to run. She was a beautiful Arabian Quarter horse, I called her "Dancer." She had an untamed spirit from not being properly broke in, and I loved her that way.

When I was around twelve years old I was baptized by my youth pastor Tim.

In Grade 6, Remi started taking me for long walks. We tried to figure out our boy problems and if my boy crushes noticed me. I needed her opinion because she knew everything about love and boys.

"So, do you think he likes me?"

"Do you talk to him?" she asked me.

"Well, every day when we pass each other in the hallway, he slams me hard and body checks me into the lockers. He plays hockey."

"Yes, I think he may like you."

My heart was aflutter.

"Well, do you really think so?"

"Yes, he definitely notices you."

"Do you think we will get married?"

"You're only in Grade 6, Joy. Your feelings are not love yet; it is infatuation."

"Well so, still."

"What happened to that other guy you liked?"

"I don't think that is going anywhere."

It seemed that everything was connected to this one, very strong emotion called love. It had the power to make me feel up or down. It lit a flame and stirred my heart. The only sightings of unicorns were the posters that hung on my bedroom walls, and I dreamed they were real. I went to bed at night thinking on those things and about the new crushes that I would like to marry, but never had the nerve to talk to.

With each passing year, the list of things to talk about grew longer, and soon, Remi and I walked the entire three-mile distance; sometimes running out of time to solve our problems of the heart.

Remi went away to Bible school in her teens. She got kicked out in Grade 11. When she came back home, our walks changed too. She kept walking all the way into town. It was some 14 miles. I begged her not to go. I walked back home alone, pretending she was with me. I felt guilty having to lie for her.

Remi's kind of love was complicated. She dated a bad boy who had a reputation for being a scraper, always getting into fights. She kept sneaking out at night, was never home, and everything in the household felt like it was falling apart.

One morning, dad turned on the lights to wake us up for school. He discovered Remi was not home. "Dallas, Joy! Did you girls know about her sneaking out?" I looked up, my dad was frantic. Remi promised Dallas and I last night that she would be back in a few hours. "No." I shrugged my shoulders and lied again.

The world was pulling Remi in one direction, and my parents were doing their best to hold on. From boys to partying, I watched her turn from my hero into someone I did not understand. I saw her choices as black. Sin. It jaded her. To me, making decisions that upset my parents were probably not good decisions. That is how I looked at things. I remained respectfully faithful on my parents' side. At night my parents tucked us into bed and went to town, looking for Remi. They were consumed with worry. It did not seem fair. Why did my parents have to check out just because Remi had?

Outside our bedroom window was a peaceful starlit night. Then came a whirlwind that started to make the long tree branches sway up and down. And I turned and looked at my sister.

"Do you think they will find her?" I questioned Dallas.

"I'm not sure. Hopefully."

"I'm worried. She is so bad now."

"Ya, I would never do what she is doing."

"She promised to be back hours ago. What do you think she is up too?"

Dallas paused a minute, looking up at the ceiling, "she is probably with her boyfriend."

"Ya. I hope they find her. I hope she gets grounded."

Life was changing fast, and I was not prepared. I closed my tired eyes, drifting off. The lightening flashed. Mighty stallions were charging across the heavens at speeds that seduced my heart. They looked magnificent. I watched; their hoofs were pounding as flint! They chased the darkness out of the sky. They raced down to the bottom of the sky and over the mountain peeks. Enormous free-standing ladders grew up from the reddish grassy earth. The ladders were an elegant sapphire colour, interchanged with rubies on the inside. I noticed the splendid and rather intricate detailing of hearts inside the metal rungs.

I began climbing, until I reached the cherished silver rope that was attached to the fin of the happiest, most adorable dolphin. It made its home in the rainbow splash clouds. It twirled and squealed, and

I stretched. It was a long reach to catch hold of the glistening rope. I clasped onto it, but only for a moment, then I decided to risk it and let go. The thrill came from the perfect ratio of a top-of-my-lungs scream, tangled hair, and wanting to do it again. I landed on the back of a lime-back whale that signalled to the dolphin, "come and play". The whale lived in a pond of a thousand yesterdays. It was filled to the brim with silky lily pads and friendly crocodiles that anyone could pet. The oak trees were a velvety marble, cascading with emerald leaves that gently waved in the breeze. The fog started to lift, and I heard my name being called. "Joy. Joy. Wake up, it's time for school sweetie."

"Five more minutes."

I was relieved to hear they had found Remi. Mom sat me down and looked into my eyes with troubling news. "Last night her boyfriend beat her up. I want to warn you. She has bruises."

"Is she okay?" I was devastated. "How could he do that to her?"

"I don't know. She will be okay, but just leave her be."

I nodded in agreement. Thankful that it would be the end of that stormy relationship. Her boyfriend had crossed the line. But when she went back to him only days later, it bowled me right over. How could she love someone who hurt her? He would do it again. How could she go back? Did she not see how much it hurt our family? She gave him chance after chance. She always forgave. And soon, I learned how to forgive too.

A few years after Remi graduated high school, she got pregnant and had a little boy, Jordan. Blonde hair, blue eyes, and the cutest little giggle. Remi was head strong and determined; torn by a tough decision. She made the right one. She left her abuser to protect her child.

It was not easy for any of us that morning to let them go. She was wounded and moving far away. Her suitcases were sitting at the door, filled with a weight of uncertainty. What things did she pack? What things did she decide to leave behind? Her tiny Chivette was not big enough to hold her past. And she headed for her future. And the bravest thing she had to do, was walk out the door and leave it all behind.

I missed them terribly and I underestimated the family dynamic. I lost a huge part of my life. I myself had no idea how one person's choices could potentially impact the next, as the road one paves makes it easier for the next to follow. My dad was always working, my mom was always worried, and my other sister was always reading books.

I spent my time ignoring the intrusions of family life. I remember lying down on the front lawn, under the heat of the summer sun, sipping the day away as if it was a Sunday. I tried to stare up at the sun, but I ended looking away quickly; it was just too bright. I was comfortable with things far away that I could admire; things felt safe, and I was way less guarded. I tricked myself into thinking those things could never hurt me. But somehow, they managed to get the closest and hurt the most.

I had Jaromir Jagr on the mind throughout my teen years. He was the constant indulgence in my conversations. He replaced my cravings for sweet, succulent sugars at Christmas time. I worked myself into a frenzy over the Pittsburgh Penguins. I was mesmerized. I took my unicorn and kitty posters down, and I put his up.

My life opened up to the game. In Grade 10, I joined the girl's hockey team, "The Silver Bullets". I had a particular cousin, who loved the Boston Bruins and hated Jagr, which made him my rival. Mom came to all my games. The star player was Mandy. We took second place from making it into the provincials, and for some unknown reason, Coach Brown called my name for MVP during my first year playing. Life was finally falling into place for me. I was beginning to find my identity.

"Hey Joy, come in here," my dad called.

He was sitting at the round table in the kitchen.

"Yes, Dad?"

"I got three tickets to the hockey game tonight. Do you want to go?"

"Are you serious?" My heart leaped. "You mean; I'm going to get to see Jaromir Jagr in person?"

Dad smiled. "I got three tickets. You, me, and Grandpa. Let's go."

"I have to get ready!"

I ran to my dad and gave him a hug. Dad knew how special this would be for me, and he was happy to do it. I was freaking out! Soon, I would be seeing Jaromir Jagr for the very first time.

I wore light-coloured jeans, and a bright red shirt. I was a very sweet sixteen. The warm-up was about to begin, and people were trickling into the Northlands Coliseum.

I went right down in front of the players' bench and waited for him there. I was nervous and wished someone was with me, like my mom, so she could enjoy this very special moment with me.

My palms were sweaty, and the building was a little chilly. The players started coming out on the ice. It felt larger then life. Oh my goodness. It was him. When he was right in front of me, he looked right at me and held my gaze. It might have been only four seconds, but it was the best four seconds of my life.

When I look back, I faced the music. If our relationship is in right standing with God, He is in the centre of our heart and mind and has our total devotion. The Lord warned me and made it very clear in a private conversation, "Who is going to challenge My Supremacy." Little children, keep yourself from idols. Amen. 1 John 5:21 Fear God. Ask Him for yourself and work it out.

Lord God, please help and keep me. I trust in You.

Grade 10. We moved back to town.

In the off-season, Dallas was hung up on a guy. It was exciting to watch her fall in love with the guy of her dreams. I witnessed gold being spun, and I hoped my turn would be next.

"Hey, Dallas. What are you up too?"

Dallas' hair was long and dyed platinum blonde. She had just come inside from uptown. She glowed from being up high, riding on the chariots of love.

"I'm getting ready to go back out with Paul."

"Oh. What are you guys doing?" I asked, sitting on her comfy little bed. I leaned into the fluffy pillows that cradled my head.

"We are going to a party."

"Really? Well, you look really good. How late are you staying out?"

"I'm not sure. I'm sure I will be back not too late."

"Okay, I will let Mom know when she asks. Have fun."

"I will." I got up and left her room and went upstairs to mine.

Red-hot romance sure changed things. This was her first boyfriend and I noticed her absence. The night passed and the sky started to fall. I don't remember how much time was in between the next time I saw her. But I can't forget it. I was sitting downstairs watching TV, and she came home crying. I couldn't remember the last time she had been so upset. I jumped off the chair and went to go check on her.

"What is wrong?"

I sat down next to her. She was lying face down, with her head buried, sobbing.

What could have happened? She was devastated.

"I found out Paul cheated on me," she finally said.

"No way."

"You guys were completely in love. How could this happen?"

I remembered both of their smiles and energy. It was first love. You could see the sparks between them. They had major chemistry.

After a long cry, she turned and looked at me, "How could he do that to me?" she questioned, heartbroken.

I felt sickened. "I don't know. I'm so sorry." I softly rubbed her back, trying to console her.

He had broken her heart. She closed the door, and things would never be the same.

Dallas moped around every day, eating mostly carrots, and her fingers turned orange. I didn't understand what was going on with her. She would tell me stories about her new friends. But they were things I considered more troubling than worth pursuing. She was headed into oncoming traffic and down the same path as Remi.

I stuck close to Mom. Dallas changed her friends, partied, skipped school, and would be gone for days at a time. The family's good times were becoming very short-lived. Any familiar sounds of love that once whirled me around in the room while my mom was playing the piano stood silent.

In our huge two-story house, it would appear to the outside world that this home was perfect. The kitchen was upstairs. The rooms were big, but the space felt ever so lonely. The halls wrapped around the staircase, which was placed in the centre of the grand home.

Mom and I were in the kitchen chopping up salad for supper. She had not been feeling well. She had thyroid troubles and stress made her weary.

"Where is your sister staying?" she asked.

I shrugged, "I don't know. I never saw her in school today. I walked down her hallway at break and lunchtime but I never saw her."

"I don't know what to do with her. Where is she all the time? Does she even go to school anymore?" she asked frustrated.

"I don't know. Don't worry, it will be okay. I would never hurt you."

We seemed to be hunted. It seemed unbelievable to think that you could have your sister one day and not even know her the next.

I did not understand how things changed overnight, and the betrayal was deep.

"Thanks sweetie. Dad and I were talking. If she wants to go to Bible school, we will send her."

When September came around, Dallas took off to a different town with new chances. Hopefully she would make it and thrive. It was a surprise to me how it felt to be an only child. There was no more worrying about what my sisters were up to. Suddenly, I was receiving way more attention. What a dream come true. Even more so, it felt like it was my turn to discover life. It had taken me my entire adolescence to figure out who I was. I found confidence when I really took a step outside myself. I finally had some incredible friends. I could go to sleep at night not worried about tomorrow. I was ready to take on the world with no one stopping me. I added two cups of certainty, three table-spoons of faith, mixed it all up with a handful of prayers, and baked it on high hopes. I turned to Mom, smiling, and tapped my finger on the end of her nose. I gave her a wink. "I promise you that it will all turn out."

Grade 11. I watched out the window, waiting for June to drive up in her parents' big blue boat. I was looking good at five feet two, with dirty blonde hair. At 8:35 a.m., June pulled up in front of my house right on time, and I headed out the door. June and Lily were sitting in the car, smiling at me.

"Good morning, chick," they said as I put my bag down and buckled in.

"Good morning." I smiled looking back at them.

June was gorgeous, had the perfect smile, figure, and was smart. Lily was another complete package. She had dirty blonde hair, beautiful eyes, and a cute wiggle when she walked – she was the sassy one. June put the car in drive and Lily cranked the tunes. "We are the Moron

Brothers, don't get along with others." Listening to NOFX, we pulled up to Shannon's house. She had bigger and browner eyes than June and was committed to her figure skating and academics.

"Good morning beautiful," June sang out.

"Good morning you guys."

By now, we were only a block from school. June put the car back in drive, turned a sharp nut, and spun the car around. We held on to anything in the car to keep ourselves in our seats.

"Whoa June, you're crazy!" we said laughing.

"Ya my dad gave me trouble about the car again. I guess I should try to drive a bit nicer. He says the car needs new brake pads, and I think I lost a hubcap that time I jumped the curb."

"You're not going to be grounded again, are you?" Shannon asked.

"Just say it wasn't your fault. You're not the only one that drives the car," Lily offered in her defence.

"Well, I have to have the car home right after school, or I'll be grounded."

"We still got lunch time!" Lily said, and we all giggled.

June parked the car, and it felt like we were arriving in style. This took us to a new level of maturity. We didn't have to walk or take a bus; we had new privilege that made us more than what we were on the outside. We all walked into school together. Our lockers were right next to each other down hallway C. Really could our lives be better than that? Just wait. We all had boyfriends at the same time!

Vaughn and I met that summer. And I was daydreaming about that boy. He had soft, brown curls tucked behind his ears. His favourite band was Bad Religion, and those baggy pants he wore said nothing about his quick wits. From the first moment I met him, I wanted him to be my boyfriend. He was a year younger and not pushy like some guys try to be.

I was up town with Lily when I first met Vaughn in the park. We sat in a circle hanging out and talking. Life was on course. Everything was falling into place. My life felt perfect. I thought I had everything I needed.

At school, us girls would come in and tell each other what we did the night before with our boyfriends. "Darren came over last night. We were in my bedroom making out," Lily said smiling coolly, caught up in her own personal rapture.

"No way! You're allowed to have a boy in your room?" I poked her in the stomach. "That would be the day if I was ever allowed to have a boy even near my bedroom."

"Ya, your parents are way too strict." Lily replied. It was no big deal.

"Well, James came over to my house last night. We were watching a movie and my dad walked in on us making out!"

Shannon laughed. "How embarrassing! Did you get in trouble?" June always got caught by her dad.

"He just gave James a really dirty look. I don't think my dad likes him at all," she said, grabbing her textbooks. "What about you, Joy?"

I looked up from my locker. "Vaughn and I watched TV. My dad kept coming downstairs and glaring at us," I said laughing. "What about you, Shannon?"

"I couldn't do anything. I was studying for a test, but tonight Terry and I are supposed to do something." She grinned, and the bell rang.

Exploring what the world had to offer looked like a neatly wrapped package. I was curious to discover what was inside. Later that evening, Vaughn and I walked through the Old Folks Path. It was the shortcut we took when he walked me home.

"Brr, it sure is chilly out. It's bag freezin." I didn't know how to respond and kept smiling.

The yellow and orange leaves were turning colours fast, falling down, and crunching under our feet. I was already yearning for summer to return. I knew how quickly the season passed, disappearing under a white blanket. We paused on the path under the tall trees surrounding us. He moved some of my long hair that the wind had blown in my face. Once we got around the corner, he held my hand. It gave me butterflies. This is what I had always wanted – a boyfriend and to feel what falling in love was all about. We approached my house. It was on the corner, and I saw Mother's car in the driveway.

"Thanks for walking me."

I was thinking about how much I loved his smile. We hugged, and I had to peel myself away.

He asked, "Give me a call later?"

"Ya, okay." I let go of his hands.

He turned around and walked back uptown. I opened the back door and hustled into the kitchen. I was surprised to see Dallas home, but I did not recognize her. What in the world had happened to my darling sister? She had gone to Bible school and came back transformed alright. She was hard looking, with a tension to her face.

"Hi," I stammered, smiling awkwardly. "What are you doing back home?"

"Hey. I got kicked out of school."

Her answer was cool as she walked past me.

"Oh, really?" I noticed her clothes were different. How could her entire style change from prep into metal grunge? I did not think she hated me, but it felt like her presence did. I sensed it. The roads she travelled on, the choices she made, the people she surrounded herself with; those things brought a shiver down my spine. This was a stranger wearing a cloak of darkness, moving down into the basement, looking to devour me next.

TWO
NEVER THE SAME

Spring fever came back. I was sixteen. I hung out with my friends, had fun and went to gigs in the city. I learned what it felt like to be packed into a mosh pit. Lagwagon and Diesel Boy were the first live bands I saw. The room and energy were electrifying. So many people crushing one another in the pit. I got kicked in the head by a random boot that was crowd surfing. My body got crushed up against the front of the stage. It was full on reckless abandonment.

School days were flying by too. With Dallas back home, she was not fitting in with the family. She rarely went to school. She had the same "rebellious attitude" as my other sister, thinking she could do whatever she wanted with no consequences. I had no clue who her new friends were. We lived in two different worlds.

I was driving with Mom down Main Street in her little Volkswagen Rabbit.

"Mom, pull over. That's Dallas!"

I was startled by her limping. "What happened to her?" She was walking turtle slow.

Mom quickly pulled the car over, and I unrolled my window.

"Dallas, get in the car."

Dallas had ditched out a few days earlier. This was about the time she usually showed up, looking a little rougher than when she had left; and I was having ambivalent feelings. She slowly opened the back door and sat down uncomfortably.

"What happened?" I asked, carefully examining her. She looked banged up and her long hair needed to be washed.

"I fell off a tower," she said, avoiding eye contact and keeping her head tilted down.

"You fell off a tower? Are you okay? What were you doing? Where were you?" I asked, shaking my head.

Mom chimed in. "We are taking you to the hospital. You can barely walk." She put the car in gear, shoulder checked, and took off while I continued questioning.

"When did this happen?" I repeated.

"A few days ago."

"A few days ago! You have been walking around like this? Wow. You're smart. You know, Dallas, your attitude is really obtuse. We worry about you all the time!" I said, turning around frustrated.

Dallas and I were close while Remi was gone. We spent a lot of time together, but after her heartbreak, things drastically shifted. I could not establish a connection with where she was. We rushed over to the hospital and waited for the doctor. Mom left the room, giving Dallas a chance to spill the beans.

"Okay! What happened?" I asked.

"I was on acid, and there were snakes everywhere. I didn't know what to do. I climbed up a twenty-foot tower, then jumped off."

My eyebrows perked up. I clenched my jaw for a second before dropping it open. "What? You jumped off?" Snakes? Wow.

"Are you serious? You jumped twenty feet? You could have died!" I panicked. "Why would you jump off?" Dallas did not say much. I could not comprehend her choices. How could living recklessly be something you pursued? She was sitting on the hospital bed, staring off, shrugging her shoulders. I did not understand why she was so distant. What had happened to her? She was looking down and then around the room, annoyed at having to wait for the doctor. She had almost died. It was clear she had lost herself. She was smashed up and could barely walk. She acted like she had the world in her hands, and that it was hers to take. Did she think that she was indestructible? Drugs were like taking a dose of death, and I was shook.

Wait till I told Mom.

There was no hiding the contempt Dallas held toward my parents. They did not know how to handle her bravado and tried to reason with her. I stood outside my bedroom, listening in the other room where no one would see.

"We just want to talk to you. Please let us in," Dad said concerned. He just wanted the chance to fix whatever was broken in her.

"I don't want to talk! Go away!" she yelled through her closed door.

She cranked up her death metal music, White Zombie *Astro Creep*, drowning out any further discussion. My parents were devastated and were standing there defeated. She was driving the knife deeper through all our hearts. I was mad at my sister for treating my parents so rudely. I went back into my bedroom and closed the door. I did not like how this made me feel. It was as if the good sparks of my life were being snuffed out. Dallas was being ripped away from her entire family. My heart felt so heavy and burdened. Why did this have to happen? Why was she so angry, and why did she hate us so much? I had no clue about any of the answers.

I grabbed the phone and called Vaughn.

"Hey, what are you up too?"

"Hey, I was just listening to some music and having some cereal," he said, chill.

"Cereal? You having your favourite Lucky Charms?"

He laughed, "No. I finished those last night. I'm having Fruit Loops."

"Oh. What CD are you listening to?"

"No Use For A Name. They got a new album; it's pretty good."

"Oh Ya? Hey, do you think I could borrow your Face To Face CD?"

"Which one?"

"The one we were listening to last time I was at your place."

He took a moment to remember, "Oh, okay, sure. So, what are you up to tonight?"

And I put it on him, "Well, things are not going so well here," I said. "My sister is back home."

"Oh Ya. How's that going?" he mused.

"Let's just say we found her strung out of her mind. Apparently, she was on acid and hurt herself really bad."

"Are you okay?" he asked caring.

I was disappointed and answered, "I don't know. I'm not sure anymore. She is not okay. Did you hear anything about this in school?"

"Nope."

"Okay. I guess I will see you tomorrow."

"Ya okay. Good night."

I never thought I would have such heavy problems. My home was *never* supposed to be broken. My sister was not well, and I really did not know what to do. She was so different. I loved her, but it was like she was a stranger. I didn't know her. She hated us. This intruder was angry and isolated herself so far away. It made me feel alone and like I had no one to turn to or trust. What happened to my friend? To my sister?

I started to wander down my own path experimenting too. Slowly, down the gateway. Not sure when my heart had become hard. It was a gradual shift, that I had never noticed. I tried smoking. It was a rush and it gave me confidence. I spent break time at school meeting new friends. From that crowd I was starting to hear lots of people were trying acid. Maybe I had it all wrong? Or maybe I started talking to the same people as Dallas. My world was pretty small. I could not help but start to think that drugs were normal to try in high school. I had stopped attending youth group and barely went to church.

Bit by bit, I forgot about the place where slimy frogs hopped around in the pond. A home once nestled with the Juliet "ribbits" and the melody of the beautiful Romeo birds.

I was with some new "friends", sly foxes. The foxes asked me, "Hey do you want to get high with us?" I did not realize their intentions. They showed up right on my doorstep. The door to the fortress of my mind. Oh this door was giant. Tall, heavy, solid wood. The stone hedge built around it stood sturdy. Should I open the door? I peeked. I was curious to see what the hype was all about.

The idea of trying acid felt thrilling, but extremely scary.

"No. I couldn't."

All the kids that were hanging around my place were high.

I thought about it some more.

Everyone else is doing it.

I made a split-second decision and went in with the crowd.

"Yes. Okay. I want to try."

I was nervous and opened the door.

The instant I took the drug though; all hell broke loose, and the enemy came in. I wanted to back out. Each passing hour, the drug unleashed its power to destroy me. It was the prelude to death's poison, doing all it could to ravage my mind in terror. It went into every nook and cranny in my mind. I curled up in the corner of the room. Everyone was tripping out and having a horrible time. There was no where to escape myself.

Seven hours later the high kept peaking. I walked into the washroom and turned on the light switch. I looked in the mirror and screamed at the top of my lungs in horror.

"Hi there. Surprise."

I shrieked.

"What is wrong?" my friends asked, laughing.

"My eyes! My eyes! My eyes! They are not mine!" I ran back into the room and hid under the blanket. What had I let inside? Never again! Being high was like being stuck in a horror movie. After one use, I felt colder as a person. Taking acid was lethal. I did not know that it could change a person so much.

A few days later I was looking for Vaughn. I wondered to myself where he was besides on my mind. He was becoming scarce. He was starting to hang out with older people that I did not know.

That night, I heard the phone ring by my bed. I grabbed it quickly before it woke up my parents.

"Hello?"

"Hey Joy," said a quiet voice that sounded shaky.

"Vaughn, why are you calling me so late?"

"Is anyone on the other line? Is anyone listening?" he asked, acting sketchy.

"No, I don't think so," I said, raising my eyebrows. "What's going on? Are you okay?"

"I don't know. I was out with some friends."

I picked up a lighter and opened up a brown box with a pretty gold and silver fabric ribbon tied around it. I took out a candle and lit it."

"Ya, okay. Well, what happened? Why are you whispering?"

"I don't want anyone to hear me."

"Well, what are you worried about?"

He was not being his normal charming self, and I was worried.

"I was with some friends...I tried speed."

Wow. This was the stuff they warned you about in school, the hard stuff. Both of us were hushed.

"What happened? What was it like?"

"There was a line on the table. I snorted it. I felt like such a loser after I did it."

He paused again for a moment. "I felt like a junkie."

There was screaming silence on both sides of the phone.

"I never want to do that again."

I looked at the flickering of the candle that cast its shadow on the wall, not sure what to do or say with our top-secret basement shiver confessions. I could tell he meant every word he said. It sounded like he had lost a piece of himself, and I bet he was not about to give up anymore.

"Well, are you going to be okay?" I asked concerned.

"Ya, my dad just come down here... I need to go."

"Okay well, I'll talk to you tomorrow. Good night."

"Good night."

I hung the phone back up and looked at the candle glowing, then blew it out.

The next day I looked for him at school, but he was not there. I called him as soon as I got home. His mom answered. "Vaughn! Pick up the phone!"

"Hello." I heard the sound of a guy who had a rough night.

"I didn't get any sleep last night. I'm never doing that stuff ever again. It was horrible."

"Okay, I will let you get back to sleep."

I hung up the phone.

Weeks passed and life simmered down. We sorted through our various scandals. I was dull to the relativity of life's choices and how every decision does matter. Everything in life can change by one single choice. And the gradual slope, is the most cunning of all.

I went out with Vaughn to go cruising around with his friends after school. We were having a great time when he looked at me and called me, "Gonamaria!" Everyone laughed, and I blushed, sitting in the back seat of the Jimmy. Oh, it was my dearest boyfriend who came up with all the nicknames for his friends, like "fire crotch", "bear balls", and so on. I didn't like it. I let it slide a few more times before I got tired of it and dumped him.

The next day I got asked out by one of his friends and said yes. But less then two days later, I missed Vaughn and wanted him back. We dated for over ten months. I broke up with the new guy to go back with Vaughn. For some reason, there was something blocking us, but I thought it would all work out. It would just take a little time. We never had any real fight the entire time we dated.

At home in my bedroom, standing in front of my cherry red wood dresser, minding my own business, when I heard Dallas knocking on my bedroom door. I opened the door. She was high as a kite. Her face was tense. Her super-charged mind was thinking a million thoughts at once. She was apprehensive and paranoid. I could feel her energy. I was uneasy. What was going on now?

"What are you on?" I asked, stopping everything, studying her every move. Was she okay? "Why are you acting this way?"

"I'm on speed," she answered.

She was tweaked out. The outward effect was apparent; her demeanour was intense.

"What's it like?" I had heard a lot of whispering about speed. Now it was here in front of me. My sister was ripped out of her mind. She was sketched out and appeared to be too high to talk. Her eyes were jumping all around the room.

At the time, you never think your choice is "that bad". There is always a way to justify the means. It is not like I woke up that day planning to try Crystal Meth. No, the five hundred other bad choices led me down this broad road to this today. One by one, I slowly let go of everything I knew was right. Things that I should have run from stood on the other side of the line that my sister had crossed. Now, was it my turn?

"It feels amazing...like you have so much energy," she paused for a moment, "and you don't want to eat on it."

I was silent. Why didn't Vaughn tell me that?

A year after we had moved, I became ten or fifteen pounds' overweight and that had fed my fears. In Grade 10 and 11, I started counting all my calories. With everything happening in my family, I did not know how to deal with problems. At one point, my lack of eating had me weighing in at my lowest at sixty-eight pounds. I mean, it was Jaromir Jagr's number, but even to me I felt that was a bit extreme, and I tried to maintain a seventy-nine to eighty-pound average. I have to admit, it was tough to keep up the mentality to deprive myself and have so little to eat. My mind was guarded at all times. I had to stay on top of it. Gaining weight was an insurmountable fear to me; I had become anorexic.

"Really? How long does it suppress your appetite?"

"Hours, days...you can go for days without eating, or even being hungry. It makes you stop eating."

Hmm. Now I really wanted to try.

"How long does it last?" I asked.

"It lasts all day."

What would be so bad about trying that? I remembered Vaughn warning me over that late-night phone call. Everything inside me was telling me, "This is not a good idea."

"Can I try?"

Inside myself I hoped she would tell me no, and that she would protect me. I watched her every move. I was uncomfortable and incredibly nervous. My internal body temperature started boiling. I regretted asking. *You can't back out. You asked. It is to late to change your mind.*

I had no clue what the word "addiction" meant until I tried speed. I snorted a line, and it was painful. It seized me instantly. A "rush" like I had never known. Intense burn! I cringed as the drugs hit my brain.

I cradled my head in my hands to absorb the shock. My eyes watered, and I threw the snorter on the mirror. Instant anxiety. I could taste the chemical. I was incredibly high. I looked around. I was in the same room, but everything felt different. I was on edge, with my senses heightened. I was aware of everything, especially of the things that were not there. I felt uncomfortable, like I needed to leave.

I entered into a new a world, wandering through unknown capillaries; and the air felt differently. It was thicker. It had a weight of heaviness that made my chest tighten. Immediately, I was introduced to arrogance and pride – facets of this drug's identity. It was there to shape me in all its twisted ways; all the ways I did not know how to shape myself. All naivety I had was there to be stolen from me; it was there to rob me of my hope, innocence, and charm. To collect my thoughts and throw them into the garbage.

When "it" talked, it was ignorant and rude. Oh, how it *hated*. It immediately took me under its cloak. It was possessive.

We walked uptown together for the first time, and it told me. *You're mine...we will be together forever. I'm your best friend. It is me and you. See how great I make you feel!*

Everything was suddenly different. When two younger girls approached me they asked, "Do you have a light?" And what was its reaction to them? It hissed! It hated them. It hates! It hates! It hates!

How stupid are those girls! Evil chuckled with a sinister laugh. *They are so stupid. They don't know anything at all.*

This drug demanded full control. It hated my mom and dad passionately and forced me to give up all my rights.

You no longer need them! This is final! It is I you cannot live without!

That girl is naive and not have a clue what is on the horizon. Like an animal, I give no thought to the consequences of my actions.

I'm suddenly consumed with hatred. A jaded knife with a butcher's eye offered me a stunning future. It guaranteed to lift me up and sit me up high. On the full moons, evil pours out a river of kerosene, drenching me in it, vowing to find me the perfect match. The cuts were always deep and twinkled affectionately in my eyes. When you walk down the street, late at night, most likely the stranger you are passing by is carefully concealing a shank behind their back, tucked neatly away. Secrets do not always seem like sin and shame until they become exposed. You bet. I wouldn't miss it. Class would have to mark me as absent.

A world turned upside down, I would never be the same girl inside. I was about to lose everything that mattered. I watched as this drug ripped my world apart. It started with Vaughn, the one closest to me. I definitely did not know how to be a girlfriend. I had never been one before. I was a kid and new at relationships. I was susceptible to making stupid mistakes, like breaking up. No more hanging out, spending time together, just listening to all the funny things that he came up with in his head. Those brown curly ringlets of his were always so soft.

It felt as if it were yesterday we were walking together in the park and around town. Sometimes it was cold and rainy out, but "jibben" was the whole point; sliding across the bright red, wet benches. I did not know where drugs led. Maybe being a bit smarter is something that happens when you are looking back.

Sitting on my bed, I pulled out a precious box where I kept my school notes from Vaughn. We passed them in the hallways every day. I kept every one in a box with a gold lid. I read them over, trying to console myself. Friends to strangers. Love was a word I regretted never telling him.

I got up and walked over to my stereo. I put a white Patsy Cline cassette tape in the stereo and pressed "play". I sat back down on my bed and started reading through my notes, while the music was playing.

"I got your picture, that you gave to me. It still looks the same, as when you gave it, dear, the only thing different, the only thing new, I've got your picture, she's got you..."

I closed my eyes, missing him terribly. *There is no way I could ever get him back now.* Seeing him that one last time uptown in front of the 7-Eleven was like driving a nail through the coffin and walking away. There was a huge hole in my heart.

One by one, I was stripped of the things I held dearest to my heart. Soon, I was regretting lots of choices. And what is proving to be true, – everything fades over time, like good looks and laundry that hangs outside on the line.

In less than two months, I was constantly chasing after dope and doing it every day. I was on a new mission. It was the biggest mistake of my life. I hated it, yet I craved it. Grade 12, three months from graduating, I dropped out of high school. I avoided my friends. I was different, and afraid of them now. I used meth and there are rules: if you used, we could be friends; otherwise, keep away. The darkness demanded unity and there was no give. The rules were absolute, with no mercy. I made friends with other users. I was sketchy, stoned, and the first to write myself off. I forgot all about the fairy tales I had spent my entire life dreaming of. Suddenly, love was not even a thought in my mind. I fell short of possessing even lacklustre qualities worthy of redemption. I was sharp and skilfully cold. I was the final sister, and Joy was gone. An evil presence took over my mind, crushing my spirit, and welcomed my soul into eternal damnation. And this was where it all went sideways. In my drug-induced nightmare, I was thrown into a dark kingdom...

...There, the Joker stood tall. He keeps me busy shovelling, and I hear him say things that don't make sense.

"Lickity split down the merrygoal bowl, if I intersesh, it is the plesh. Keep digging!"

"I found another one! A jumbo night crawler! This one is huge!" I yelled out bragging.

Keep digging! The Joker laughed.

The nights were long and lonely.

I listened for any sounds on the other side of the door as I tripped out. I watched for shadows and creeping noises. I don't notice how truly lonely I had become. I hid away in constant fear from family and the reality of life. Since when did I need this? But it tells me I do.

The next day I woke up, my body hurting – perhaps from the constant stress of shovelling. Before I had clarity, evil was right there, condescending.

You need to get high! You need more! You have to get more!

There was not a moment of peace that passed my way. My head is a mess. I looked around the room and down at the empty flap sitting next to an old broken light bulb. I had finished all my drugs the night before.

I picked up a razor blade and start scraping. It only amounted to crummy fibres, but it was all I had, so I snorted that, hoping to feel like something other than a loser.

I went out searching and ignoring the terrifying regret that begged me to come to my senses. The hold was ruthless. Thoughts of leaving the darkness behind when it tells me it has become my only friend makes me despair. "Why would I want to do that?" I wandered around with its schemes, not knowing that a noose was tied around my neck, hidden from my sight. Calamity was hungry for me, and the ravens were waiting for the great day of dread, when my dead body would be the promised feast.

I walked through the bronze gates of death, and I sat down with an enemy, whose life's work was attacking me. We did a toast together. After all, he had come to plunder my house and we celebrated those misgivings. We might also do a merry dance, depending how the rest of the evening unwinds. It's sure to be full of doom, gloom, brilliant highs, just so he can make me crash, oh, so low. I get so excited. I can barely wait! I know its voice. It sounds like injustice, taking me as close to death as it possibly can. I hold a counterfeit bill. I look down at it and flip it over, rolling it up, believing it's worth more than my life, and I throw it away.

I walked down the dreary streets, craving drugs. The beautiful bright world around me was faded out and shoddy. Life was something I could care less about. I set off wandering after pyramids in the greatest skies or any trouble that brewed.

I wore a white undershirt, and my sneakers were black and white 'Simple'. My hair was long and beautiful. I had dyed it platinum blonde. My eyes were now black and doped up and a greasy film covered my face. I looked down at my ripped Levi jeans. What was I doing? How could I get some money? The quickest solution was my parents' gas card. I mean, it was easy enough. I knew where it was, and I had the code for it. I was thinking I could get forty bucks, maybe sixty, something that they wouldn't really notice, something "forgivable".

I hit up Frank Maddock High School and ran into Zac. He was tall and had dark hair. I had once hit him with my car in the school parking lot.

"Hey man, I got a question."

"Okay?"

"Well, I have a gas card. Would you help me sell some gas and make some money?"

The steps were small, but the void felt tremendous.

"Sure, let's go to the parking lot and see who's around."

Zac lined up vehicles. To my dread, they kept coming one after another. The pit of my stomach grew. This was not what I had in mind. Standing there I felt so alone. I could not help but ask myself where was Vaughn? I missed him. I never saw him anymore. My good old friends were in school.

What was I doing? How could I do this to my parents? It didn't take long to rack up the damage on the gas card. $700 just over lunch. I stood there the entire time, wishing I could stop what was going on, but I did not say a word. At this point, I was ready to get out, but I took my money instead and went and got high. I could not enjoy being high after what I had done. I hated myself now.

I sat in a car, watching three guys tripping out over changing a flat tire. It reminded me of the three stooges. I was lost for hours. At times, it seemed like the stooges were in fast-forward, going around in circles, making me laugh! I gazed out the window, looking up into the sky, zoned out. I had never seen it like this before. A giant mystery, wrapped up in the clouds. It was fascinating – bright hues and deep saturation. I had never seen such colours before. In no time, I begin to slowly come back down. Once again, I felt painful regret.

Zac said, "Hey, let's go back to town and sell some more gas!"

I was infuriated. What a jerk. I was pretty sure I had ripped my parents off enough. But it wasn't enough; it never is. I turned on them, sitting in the back seat. His comment triggered shotguns going off in my mind. I was trailblazing through a sidewinder of delusions that made me feel as though I should throw him down on the ground. I wanted to take razor blades to his chest and slash him over and over, until all this newfound hate of mine could be ejected from my soul. Holding the gas card in my hands, I folded it in half until I heard it snap. Then I folded it again and heard it again, "snap, snap." We were driving down the highway, around town, passing by UFA Petroleum. I rolled down my window, took the broken card, and tossed it outside the window as we drove. I was thankful.

Nonchalantly, I looked around the vehicle, wondering if anyone noticed. The breeze coming in through the window felt cool on my face, giving the utterance of something that felt real. I hated the feeling of coming back from somewhere I did not belong. My face was as blank as my stare. I looked down at my hands, holding nothing except each other. After throwing out the gas card, I felt relief that I would not be able to hurt my parents anymore. It was the only thing I had done right in a long time.

Zac looked over at me and asked, "Did you break that gas card?"

I looked at him. I was cold and nodded yes.

"Why?" He glared at me from the passenger side.

"Because, it was enough."

His eyes were dark and remote. I thought maybe I was just staring back at my own reflection, but it was not that. There was so much more underneath. Maybe it was pain? And I looked back out the window, a lost soul.

I made friends with a girl named "Easy E". She was pretty. She had beautiful bright blue eyes and was a brunette. She picked a little and it left scabs on her face. I had never seen her at school before. She wore tight clothing and heels. We used together and found people to try and rip off. I learn to lie, hate, and steal. It seemed to come naturally. After a few sleepless nights, I started shaking.

"I can't handle this," I told her. "I need sleep." My head and mind began caving under the pressure of sleepless nights. I was at a random hotel, where friends were hanging out. We all had insomnia. I knew one guy from school named Dakota. He always wore a bandana and was thin. We stayed in a hotel room above the bar.

Every night we heard loud music. We stayed in Journey's room. This guy was slowly losing his mind. Journey was a bouncer at the bar. Every night when Journey finished work, he came back up to his room. We all sat around and got high.

As the weeks passed, we all noticed that Journey never slept. He was up for an entire month. He started talking about crazy things, and we didn't know who he was angry with.

Me and Dakota looked at each other, and Easy gave me an uncomfortable look. This guy was unstable and was clearly getting aggravated. He was ranting and accusing everyone. Journey started screaming and we heard sirens.

We split down the stairwell fire escape as the police came.

The officer pulled up to me and asked, "Hey. Do you want a ride home?"

Easy clasped onto my arms, drawing me close into her, "No, she is coming with me."

Officer White looked back at me. I want to go with him and reluctantly tell him, "No, I will be fine. Thanks."

Life was suddenly hard. I knew I was on the wrong path. I missed my parents. I thought I did not deserve their forgiveness – that much was obvious. I thought I deserved to be punished for being so cruel. I remembered what my sisters had put my parents through. I despised myself for acting the exact same way, and a hundred times worse. I felt defeated and alone. I seemed unable to gain the upper hand. My parents had chased after Remi and Dallas, and for both girls, it was to no avail. I was waiting for them to come rescue me, but they did not come for me like they had for my sisters.

A soul crushed at seventeen. It was so shaming. I tried to escape it, but I could not defeat it. The anger and rage I felt was inexpressible. It wanted to overpower me and all those around me. Evil is spiritual, so it needs people to enter into our earthly realm. People will do evil's destructive work for Satan. And I could not defy it. It raged on anything that dared separate us.

Dallas had taken off with her boyfriend to Queen Charlotte Island and left my world in chaos. Now I spent my evenings alone, and I ached for my friends. I cared about graduating, and I began realizing I had made some major mistakes. I was only three months' shy of my most important achievement. It had taken me years to find my place, and to give it all up made no sense. Man, I know trauma is not only found in the ER. I bred trauma like I bred puppies – for the fun of it. Pissed.

I was counselled with nonsense from a serpent that guided my travels through tunnels, twisting around the rocks. I had plunged down into a dark ravine. So long ago, a boundary existed between the light and the darkness, but I could not even see that anymore. What remained in my thoughts was a shadow of a life ebbed away. I lay awake at night in ruins. The soil was not so sweet, and neither was the rest.

Sometimes you don't know how near evil actually is. It comes closer than you can imagine. Then one day, it is staring you right in the face. I was the perfect carrier. You would never suspect that such a sweet, innocent girl could inflict the sharpest of pain. If I made you feel safe for a moment, good. You wouldn't see it coming. Whether it was stealing my mom's jewellery or breaking into the church office and stealing money from the secretary. I had turned from a charming girl into a wild animal that no one stopped. So, at nineteen, I had to do something to save myself. I packed my bags. I was desperate to escape. I dared not look back. My soul depended on it.

I drove out of town and into thick, sweet-smelling pine trees. The tall grass waved goodbye at me the entire drive. I passed over the North Saskatchewan River from Alberta, and the pace just felt different. Within its borders was a peaceful haven waiting.

I checked into Nipawin Bible College. My grandparents had paid for my first year. There was no good reason for my life to have gone so off track. I sang along with the time lines written in the holy hymnals, and I worshipped His Majesty. I had no diagnosis for what I was to do. My heart and mind were badly damaged. It had been deeply betrayed. I needed major healing within. I was spiritually blind. I had eyes that could not see, ears that could not hear, and a heart with no understanding.

While I was there, I went for long walks and talked to Jesus. I longed for more of Him. I loved Jesus, but I was so lost. I was desperately trying to find myself again in all the ways I did not know how. I wanted to be made whole. The search for the truth took me a journey to find.

The season wound up, and the question arrived; what now? There was a posting on a billboard that advertised room and board in exchange for help with home renovations. I looked into it and met Cindy. The door opened. I moved upstairs into her charming house in Tisdale, Saskatchewan.

I walked into a small town that was new to me, and once again, I never bothered to discern my actions. How could I forget? No, this package looked different. It was still early on in life, and I had no sense where my choices led. I was blind. I walked and walked. My family was too far away to know any different. I could go anywhere I wanted. I could make any choice I wanted. I was lured in. There was no stopping excitement from persistently tapping me on the shoulder and inviting me to come. Once again, I turned around to see who was there. Oh, it was just fleshly desires, dressed to the nine's.

I stayed and I strayed from such a lovely Lord, and once again, things start going wrong.

I was twenty years old when I found a job at a 7-eleven, and I met Justice. He was boyishly cute and possessed endearing qualities. He was staying at an old abandoned house outside of town. We started hanging out.

"You know Joy, 'Justice' is not my real name." I looked over at him.

We were driving down Main Street. The comment caught me off guard.

"What are you talking about? As if that is not your name," I said, studying his face then looking back at the road and turned down the music.

"It's not. There is a warrant for my arrest, so I changed my name."

"Then what is your real name?" I asked skeptically.

"It's Larry."

I laughed and rolled my eyes at him. "I don't believe you," I said, twinkling at him.

The only thing I could get out of him was a mischievous smile. Justice was proud of the fact he was a BC boy, and his past – well, he did not like to talk about it. Justice finally moved into a place in town. I opened the door to the building that was condemned. The guy who lived in the basement was an older drunk who popped pills. I went up to Justice's place. In the hallway, I could hear voices coming from inside the room. I knocked on the door. "Come in," Justice yelled, and I opened the door.

It was cramped. Smoke and sunlight lingered within the tightly fitted room. I felt awkward with a bunch of guys being there. I looked at Justice. He was my bro. I wondered where these people had come from. I notice one guy in particular when I took my place next to Justice. He stood out. His look screamed anger, and like he was headed down the wrong path. That was blatantly obvious. Tattooed across his stomach was the word "demon". The guy had no shirt on. His hurt and pain looked excruciatingly deep, and it troubled me.

In my blindness, I did not understand. I know God loves him tenderly. In ways the broken do not realize. God knows the heart can see the hurting. Having tattoos is not going to stop God from wanting to have a relationship with us. God wants to embrace us. The more pain we have, the deeper the hole we can dig. I turned to the world to numb my pain. God wants our void spaces and to fill the emptiness we feel inside. Sit with silence for a month or so. If you push the world out, you will know what you have let into your being. And you need to know. Truth be told, endowment's can be so unusual. The hole inside us becomes our portion, and now the portion has been doubled. Pain can be a gift that we do not know what to do with; until we take it to The Lord. He turns the impossible pain into His glory. He fills our cups. They will overflow with that much more love from the King.

I looked at Justice, very apprehensive.

I pulled him to the other room, away from the crowd.

"Who are these guys?" I whispered, unnerved. "Dude...they look kind of evil. Did you see that guy's stomach?"

"Ya, I know." Justice smiled at me, kind of chuckling. "That guy is on probation for doing a home invasion. He stabbed an old man and cut off some of his fingers I heard."

"Man, what are they doing here! Let's ditch em' and go uptown."

"Agreed." I followed him back to the other room.

"Okay guys, we are going uptown, so I gotta bail."

The guys looked us up and down and then got up and left. I turned to Justice as soon as the guys were gone.

"Okay Justice, how do you know these guys?" I was protective over him.

"I needed some weed, and I met the one guy at the bar." He grinned, shrugging his shoulders. The light from the window shined bright in his eyes.

"Wow," I said, rolling my eyes, laughing. "So, how is the weed?"

"It's okay. Ya, they are kind of sketchy," Justice said laughing.

I was not going to allow apparent trouble to walk right back into my life. I was my own person, free from hard drugs. I moved out and rented my own house. I got my GED. I started going to SIAST College to get my Accounting and Computer Works Certificate. Even though math had been my worst subject in school, I was working to pass a tough course. It felt good. I was sober. I had a friend who cared. Life felt really good again.

And that is when I met Jimmy.

He was the life of the party. He had no qualms about speaking his mind, and he was confident. He had bright green eyes and strawberry-blond hair he tucked under his hat. His personality was more like an intense kick drum heartbeat. High, enthusiastic energy; he always had a grin on his face. He had a tiny gap between his front teeth. At first, I thought he was overly loud.

Across the road from my house stood a giant tall bee. The bee was the welcome mascot for the town. One evening, Jimmy and I climbed up on top of my roof to gaze at the stars. Frogs were croaking in a nearby pond. The breeze was calm and tenderly rustled the nearby trees. The stars held up the sky in serenity.

He opened up right away. "I used to play hockey."

"Oh really. For how long?"

"Years. I even went down to Minnesota to an NHL training camp."

"Wow, you must have been pretty good. So why would you quit?"

"I wish I hadn't. I would have made it. My mom stopped coming to watch my games, and it made me mad, so I stopped playing. I was playing for her. But now I wish I hadn't stopped."

"Well, why did she stop watching you?"

Jimmy looked down, clenching his other fist. "Her boyfriend was more important. So, I started hanging out with those guys, doing drugs, drinking."

He looked the other way for a moment, hesitating, then looked back down and continued. "It messed everything up for me."

I came to know he was good friends with the guy who had the demon tattoo. All his secrets made me protective of him. Underneath, it sounded like he was lonely and needed love. It never seemed right or fair. His childhood had been stolen for him. Deep down, he needed that one special thing that grows from out of the heart. Love. You don't always notice when it blooms, but when that lightening strikes, you sure feel it.

People were chirping about the new lovebirds in town.

Justice came over, wearing a black shirt that covered his bio-hazard tattoo on his chest and khaki pants with lots of pockets.

"Hey Joy, I went to a party last night."

"Oh really? How was it?" I ask, throwing a bright-green hoodie on and tucking my hands in the front pocket.

"Um, it was okay. They were talking about Jimmy and his ex-girlfriend."

"Oh really? What were they saying?"

"I heard Jimmy is a psycho."

"What?" I raised my eyebrows and batted my eyelashes at him a couple of times before shaking my head. "Justice, Justice, Justice, what am I going to do with you? You sure don't beat around the bush. Who said that?"

"Everyone says that," Justice exclaimed prophetically. "I really don't think you should date him."

I stood there stunned.

"I guess he punched his ex-girlfriend in the face a few months ago."

"What? You must be joking. No way." He looked at me, straight-faced and serious. Whatever he had heard the previous night he had come over first thing to tell me.

"Well, Jimmy is extremely caring and loving to me. Look, he just bought me this golden locket. Isn't it beautiful?"

"Why did he buy you that?" he asked, examining it closer.

"He got it for me when I passed that accounting course at school. Can you believe it?" I said. "Besides, you guys were all drunk last night anyhow. They probably don't remember saying those terrible things."

Justice turned and sat down on the chair, giving me a worried look that made me feel uneasy.

"Come on. You know Jimmy. He is a pussycat! Well, maybe more like a tiger. Grrrrrrowl," I said and burst out laughing.

"Shut up," Justice said, smiling at me, shaking his head and pointing his finger. "Okay, but I warned you."

Woe. His words were like splashing lava on my soul, scolding and hot, like care I needed. I looked into his eyes, secretly fearing what he had said was true. Why did I have to have these feelings for Jimmy?

I rested my forehead against my hand. He had a strong hold on me. He stood ten feet tall in my eyes. No skyscrapers or man-made walls, no dungeons or trap doors. I held not a weapon in my hand, and what beat inside of me was an unconditional heart.

"Okay," I admitted. "Maybe I noticed he has a little temper. But it is toward guys and only when he drinks. I'm sure things will be fine," I said, shaking my head and looking up.

A deep, murky, sinking feeling inside myself revealed emotions that I did not want to believe. "If he does anything to me, I will just break up with him."

Justice sat there looking at me. He feared for his friend.

THREE

CONNED

Jimmy moved in with me and the booze began to flow. I fooled myself in spite of the warning. The coffee table was covered with liquor bottles, and my life took another turn in a way I never intended. Yes, it was fun to have a good time, but this was not what settling down looked like to me.

Jimmy and his friends were jammin' late into the night. Jimmy was in the other room. I could hear him laughing blissfully; his mood elevated by the booze. His eyes were glazed. "There's a bad moon on the rise." And boy, that could not be closer to the truth.

We travelled down back alleys to pick up weed and came right back. Jimmy opened the fridge to grab a beer, only to find out it was missing. "Who was here? Who took my beer?" His bright green eyes flashed with anxiety. I rushed over. Sure enough, his beers were gone. In minutes of his friends talking, Jimmy figured out it was Stan.

"Come with me," he said.

Outside of Stan's place it turned into a long night. I felt like a vulture hovering around the trailer, but I wanted nothing other than to go home. The dawn started peaking through, and one of the guys yelled, "I'm in!" and unlocked the front door.

I walked into the trailer, feeling like an intruder, as guilty as Stan.

"You stole my beer!" I heard Jimmy yelling.

I walked down the hallway into Stan's bedroom where Stan was now hostage, lying on his mattress on the floor.

"No man! I didn't! I swear!" Stan cried out, holding his hands in front of his face to protect it.

It really didn't matter what Stan had to say, the beer was sitting right there. But this was getting blown way out of proportion. You could see Stan was sorry, and the situation was escalating.

"I'm sure he got the message, you guys, that's enough! Stop! Let's go." I yelled at the guys and looked down at Stan. He was defenceless and held himself in the fetal position.

I grabbed Jimmy's arm and pulled him out of the room. I thought Jimmy was right behind me, following me, when I heard Stan cry, "No please!"

What was going on? I turned as fast as I could back into the room. I screamed at Jimmy, "No!" Jimmy's vein in his forehead was popping out. His lean body was tensely ripped. He had a bat and was ready to knock Stan out of the park. He towered over Stan with fierce hate, then struck him – once, twice...

"No! Stop!" I lunged in and pried the bat out of his hands. I took Jimmy out of the room and out of the trailer, ignoring the cuffing that followed us down the corridor.

"What is wrong with you? What is in your lunatic head? What are you thinking?"

Jimmy couldn't disguise the phantom I saw roam behind his eyes. And like glass shattered on the ground, everyone went in their own direction.

I drove back alone to my place, questioning everything. That was brutal. I had never seen anything like it. I got home and curled up on my couch, wanting to find some warmth. I heard sirens getting closer. It was a small town and the police new everyone.

"Great." I jumped up and met the officer on the front step.

"Joy, what happened?" the officer said, rushing up to me. "Is Jimmy in there?"

I shook my head. "No. I don't know where he is."

"Were you over at Stan's place?"

"Yes."

He looked tensely at me. "Who had the bat?"

I stood in silence. Thinking over in my head what happened, I shrugged my shoulders while looking off in the other direction.

"I don't know," I said in his defence. I hated being in this position.

"Please, I need to know. Was it Jimmy? I need to know, Joy, and I know you know."

I stood on my front step in silence, looking around and staring off. The cop stood there looking at me and continued pressing, pressing, putting the pressure on.

"Ya, it was."

He looked me in the eye and nodded. "Thank you," he said solidly, like it meant a lot to him. Then he rushed back to his cruiser and took off. This time, there were no sirens.

Jimmy called me later on in the day, waking me up. I had been expecting him to come over, not a phone call.

"Where did you go after? The police came to my house asking me questions. I didn't know what to say," I quickly told him.

"I went to my grandma's house. The police showed up and arrested me," he said, sounding like he needed some answers. "What did you tell them?"

"They arrested you? You're in jail?" I said surprised.

"Yes."

"Well shouldn't Stan be in jail? He is the one that broke into our place," I said confused.

"No. Stan is in the hospital," he said factually. Then he took a sigh before asking, "Did you tell him I used the bat?"

"Oh my goodness. He is in the hospital? Seriously? Is he okay?"

"I don't know. He got beat up pretty bad. Hopefully he won't remember anything. So what did you tell the cops?"

"Well..." I stammered. "I didn't know what to say. You took off, and you didn't tell me what to do. I didn't know where you went. What were you thinking?"

I played it back in my head. Only hours earlier the cop was frantic with concern, and to be truthful, the cop's strong emotions had gripped me.

"When the cop asked at first, I said, "I didn't know." I explained how I tried to not throw him under the bus, before admitting that I actually did. I continued on with a gentle let-down.

"Oh." I could hear him shaking his head, confirming the dread of his worst nightmare.

"You shouldn't have told him I used the bat! I could be locked up for a few years because of this!"

I couldn't believe it. This all of a sudden felt like it was my fault.

"This is assault with a deadly weapon! I could be charged with attempted murder."

"What? Are you serious? Attempted murder? What? Well man, what were you thinking using a bat? Who uses a bat? Don't be mad at me. You shouldn't have used a bat. It's your own fault," I said impulsively. Looking back, maybe that wasn't the best thing to say to a person. He was silent for a minute.

"You're right. It's not your fault. It is mine. I'm sorry. I guess we will have to wait and see," he finished.

The next time I saw him he was sitting in court wearing a pale-white, long-sleeved shirt. I heard the extent of his rap sheet. It was long, and I was not impressed. I stared at him across the room, knowing what was going on in both our minds. Two very sorry people, both filled with a world of regret.

He was sentenced a year and taken away before my very eyes. I was devastated. I loved him. Would it be such a mistake if I waited for him? Him being gone made me miss him so much more. Something was telling me I needed to let him go. After seeing his explosive temper, it felt like a ticking time bomb that inevitably would blow up in my face. I knew what I needed to do. I sat outside on my front step, taking the call from jail.

"Hey, how are you?"

"I'm okay. I miss you baby." I missed him too.

"I'm sorry, Jimmy. I think we should break up."

"No. Sweetheart, why do you say that?"

I paused.

"I was not raised with partying, and you have a very bad temper. I don't think this relationship is going anywhere."

"No, babe. I don't want to break up. I love you."

"I don't think this is going to work."

"Please, Joy, you don't think I regret what I did. I will never do anything like that again. I learned my lesson."

I didn't say anything. Letting go was becoming harder than I thought. He loved me – could I turn my back? I loved him too.

"Do you think I like being away from you? I hate it. I would never do anything to be separated from you again. Please, it will be different."

What he was saying kind of made sense. He was swaying me.

"Well, I don't know. I will think about it."

"Joy, I'm stuck in jail. I need to know you will wait for me. I would do anything to go back and do it over again. I never thought I would find a girl like you. I can't lose you. You're a part of me."

I was convinced. "Okay. I will wait for you. I love you. I will talk to you tomorrow."

"Okay baby, I promise this will never happen again. I love you."

"I love you too."

I got off the phone and sat alone in our empty house. I should have stopped talking to him completely. I should have shut him out of my life and made a break for it while I had the opportunity. It was golden. I was fooling myself to think I had any control in this situation.

No letter could be sent, no picture drawn, no pill dosed, no prescription filled. No tranquilizer shot up; could cure the pain within.

Letters started to come to the post office box daily. I was faithful and wrote him back. Words are words. People can say anything, nice things, all the things you want to hear, all the things that work their way straight into your heart. Anything is possible with the perfection of a master manipulator. Soon there was no doubt left in my mind, and I went to visit him.

It was not hard to figure out which big building was the Correction Centre. High towers, raised fences, and razor-wrapped barbed wire along the top were enough to give it away. This should have caught my attention and been a red flag warning "danger". This was not the picture I dreamed of as a little girl – going to meet my boyfriend in jail.

I followed along the road until I came to the front entrance. I walked in with a glowing tan, wearing a summer dress and shimmer-pink lip-gloss. I tried to keep my balance and not wobble in my heels as I approached the reception desk – "click, click, click". I felt insecure. I had never been in a jail before. The guard came up to me. The first thing I noticed was his sidearm. It made me nervous.

"What is a girl like you doing in a place like this?" he asked.

"I came to visit my boyfriend."

"What is your boyfriend in for?"

"Assault."

"On you?"

I smiled. I was obliviously stupid. "Nope, not on me."

"Well, I'm glad to hear that." He checked me over, and I proceeded to a small room. Jimmy was sitting there and on his best behaviour. What a relief to see him again. No doubt, I was very easily attached. I sat down and he took my hands. They felt cold and clammy.

"How are you?" I studied his face intensely. His eyes were bright against the paleness of his complexion. I missed his smile, and his energy was something I was used to now.

"I'm doing okay. I miss you," he said, smiling at me. "I love seeing you. Thanks for coming." He smiled again.

"You look pale. Are you getting beat up in there?" He looked down for a second, then back up, smiling brightly at me.

"No, I'm not getting beat up," he chuckled. "And I'm pale because I don't get hardly any sun." He started to frown for a second.

"I picked you some flowers. I pressed them in the letters I sent you. Did you get them?"

"Yes. I got them," he said laughing and gave me a wink.

"Have you seen my sister?"

"Ya. She is still crazy. I ran into her in Nipawin and I picked her up." Jimmy smiled. "What was she doing?"

"Well, she was still drunk from being on a 4-day bender. I guess she smashed into a pole and wrote some guys truck off."

"That's Connie for you."

"No like. We were driving back down the highway and she unrolled the window and climbed out. She was standing on the window ledge- while I was driving full speed."

"What did you do?"

"I yelled at her. I told her she was crazy and to get back in the car before she killed herself! I was so mad at her."

"Ya, she needs to quit drinking."

"Tell me about. This sucks you're missing summer. I want you home so badly. Thanks for the letters, and pictures baby. You spill your heart on the pages. It is beautiful. You have this ability to make me feel so special. Soon you will be out. I can't wait to put this behind us."

"I love you."

"Love you too."

By luck, Jimmy got out of jail on my birthday. It was a beautiful summer day out in front of the local courthouse. I had waited for him an entire year. The night before he was released I hardly slept. What a long wait. I darted straight and aimed for his heart. I never missed. I jumped in his arms and stayed for a few moments.

"Here," he said, "I got this for you." He handed me a box. I opened it. It was a beautiful gold ring. It had a heart and three diamonds. Plus, he had a dozen red roses for me. He made me feel incredibly special. Time was back in our hands. There were no more guards listening in or watching us.

He was on house arrest and not allowed to leave. We walked home and sat down.

"Let me feel your body," I said, ravishing him. "Let me make sure you are really here. Do not move." I touched his chest, felt his arms, absorbed his presence, and instructed him further. "Just keep smiling. Let me see you smile." He grinned really big. "Take irons and chains and wrap them around us. The heavier, the better. I never want to go through that ever again."

"Baby," he replied dramatically, "I would die a million cold unendurable winters if it meant I would see your face after it was all over."

"How could anything be better than love?" I replied.

"Baby, your halo shines. You're a vision of more than my dreams. Thanks for waiting for me."

"Babe. Just hold me close. Promise me you won't let go."

I held him so tight, not wanting to let go of him again.

"Baby... I won't ever let you go," he said back.

"I love you."

"I love you so much too."

Right there everything felt so right. Emotions and tears started filling up my eyes.

"It was the worst being apart from you."

We were both grateful. I never wanted to go through that again.

Months passed. We crossed the days off the calendar; soon house arrest would be over. Things shifted. We never discussed mortgages. I told him what I wanted out of life and he agreed. And yet, we found ourselves doing the exact opposite. I guess one of my problems were the lies. How easy it is to live them. And how easily I believed them.

The chaos of a life once lived and lost was easy enough to gradually pick back up. His freedom seemed to bring flashes of uncertainty and chaotic madness.

I was sitting down in our living room. I was happy. I thought we had a good evening. The walls were holding everything up. No dead bodies had been buried in the back yard. The only skeletons were from past lives that I could never bury.

Our place was tidy. We had two couches, a coffee table, plants, and a ridiculous stereo system. Jimmy was in the kitchen, standing across from me eating. I was hungry too. It was late at night.

"Can I have a bite of your sub?" I asked.

He stopped eating and shot me a death glare.

I felt uncomfortable. What did I do?

He demanded, "Why didn't you get a pizza sub at the store? I asked you if you wanted one?"

"Sorry... I didn't want a whole one. I just wanted a bite of yours."

"Here. Have the whole thing!" The sub flew across the room, hitting me, and fell apart. I was speechless. I wanted to disintegrate into the couch. He started pacing and went on a bloody rant about something so much more than our evening. I don't play guessing games. And I watch him start to annihilate the room.

He was like a guard dog, but why was I the enemy? I thought he loved me. So why would he turn on me? Now, I was the one locked behind a tall fence and feeling caged. Being held back didn't stop him from foaming at the mouth and chomping at the bit. I didn't understand. I held out my hand, offering loving gestures and a master's soothing voice. But it was like he had rabies. I looked around the room, watching him turn everything upside down. I began to realize that my worst fear had come true. I had been conned.

I sat back, tense. He started scaling the fence. I begged him to calm down. I shut my eyes, bracing with fear. I did not know how horrific it was going to be. His blood must have been boiling the whole time while he was locked up in jail. It got clearer and clearer that he was angry, and I was going to pay.

I tried to get away; I ran into the bedroom and slammed the door. I didn't know what to do; there was no escape. He kept hammering on the door. It was only a matter of time before he forced his way in.

"Please stop! Please stop...please, please. No no no no no no no no no no no no no no."

Jimmy was filled with rage and grabbed me. He threw me down and screamed at me. He spat on my face. I never felt so humiliated in all my life.

I was never haunted, until that moment. Our ghost ship set sail on that night into the stormy, uncharted seas. I store this memory in a closed-off room in my mind. No one can get in or out. I just never thought I would be locked away with it, and that he held the keys. The room was small with just one small window. No light reflected into the room.

He reached up to the top of my closet and pulled out my special box – the one with the gold lid. I was horrified. This guy was going too far. He could do whatever he wanted to me, but he could not touch my letters from high school. Oh, no. He started opening them up. He was irate that I had them. Is this the reason why he was mad at me?

Those letters were incredibly important. They represented a time I could never get back. Those were my last memories before the drugs. They were harmless times of my youth and innocence, before it was stolen from me. He ripped them into hundreds of pieces and turned the room upside down.

I pleaded for his mercy, but he showed me none. Unlawful confinement. All night long. I guess he wanted to show me what jail was like. When he was finished, he sat back, cleaning himself. Then he came over to me and lovingly started licking my wounds.

The next day, I sat up in bed. The room was silent. I looked around the room. Everything was tidy and, in its place, – as if nothing had happened. I hated him. I listened if I could hear him; it was still. Wait! I think I hear something! I was trembling with fear. I quickly lay back down. I pretend to be sleeping. I felt him come into the room. Oh no. He was sitting on my bed... I tried not to move.

"Are you up?" he said in a soft, sweet voice.

I felt him gently caress my hair away from my face. I slowly opened my eyes. What! Was he serious? My anxiety went through the roof. I felt trapped. Afraid. I had no idea what could happen next! Strangulation? Stabbing? Suffocation?

I got up and walked straight out the front door with Jimmy following behind me. I sat on the front step and lit up a cigarette. I felt like I could run if I had to.

"I do not want to be with you. Not after last night. I can't be. You need to leave."

"Joy, I'm so sorry. I don't know what happened to me. I think I need medication to control my temper. I really do not know what I'm doing."

Jimmy took it slow, like he had heard it a million times before.

"I'm so sorry to put you through that. I know it is wrong. It should never have happened. I love you. I don't want to lose you. Please forgive me. I'm sorry. I will never do it again."

I never said anything. I was traumatized. This was not love. I was exhausted and had no energy left. The life had been sucked out the night before. Like any addiction, it leaves you drained.

"I'm sorry. Here, I got this for you." He gave me a small box. "Open it."

"I don't want it."

"Here please, just look at it. Please."

He opened it up. It was a very beautiful necklace with a heart.

"Joy, I'm so sorry. I will never do that again. I got this for you to show you how sorry I really am."

Jimmy pulled the necklace out of the case.

"I'm sorry. Please forgive me. Please give me another chance. I will get on medication and go see a doctor. When I get on the medication, it will fix me. I will be better. I need you. I promise, I won't do it again."

Give me the rise of the sun and the promise of another day that I will feel your love remaining in my heart. I did not think love was easy, but I did not imagine it ever being this hard. Do not add me to your list of casualties. You knocked people down one at a time. But you had knocked me down more times than I bothered to count. You hurt me you know... Did you notice me broken and crying on my knees? You were crushing my spirit, you know... Did you notice me begging for mercy? Well, if you did happen to notice, I was caged and lived in fear. Your love was a tempest, crushingly deranged. I didn't think I could survive your fury. But the best thing about all of this was that it was "all my fault" because I stayed.

Like a carousel, the cycle of abuse went around and around. I went to work, trying to hide the bruises. I got tired of making up excuses to tell concerned co-workers when they asked, "What happened?" No matter how many times anyone told me to leave, I didn't. My mind wandered around with him on the foolish cycle he led me on. He manipulated my emotions and preyed on my fear and vulnerability. Control a person's emotions, you can control their mind.

Months passed and the fighting continued, spiralling out of hand. I needed someone in my corner. I called my sister Remi and her husband Ken to get Jimmy out of my life. What a relief that they only lived a town away. They were always there for me.

Ken was a husky guy, with a heart of gold. He was Prince Charming, who rode into Remi's life in a mighty silver Thunderbird. He truly swept Remi off her feet and into his loving, protective arms. When Remi had left town all those years ago, she was determined to make a life for herself. By doing the right thing, God put her life back together. And now, I needed them both. Well, Ken had no problem telling Jimmy what he thought.

"You're lucky I didn't bring a truck full of guys with me. We would have taken you somewhere that no one would ever find you again, and no one would care!"

Wow, these guys from Saskatchewan sure were blunt. Jimmy said nothing, and Ken was not joking.

"This is my little sister, and no one hurts my little sister! You need to get your things and leave her alone! Don't call her. Don't try and talk to her. It is over."

I thought for sure Jimmy would shrink back. But that is not the case. He was defiant.

"It is really none of your business," Jimmy shot back.

His cheekiness probably took Ken by surprise. It sure did me. And the room was heated.

"It is my business when you hurt my little sister! Now get your things and go!"

Ken and Remi started helping him pack his stuff. Jimmy called his grandma to pick him up. And like that, he was gone.

"Are you okay, Joy?" Ken and Remi asked.

Remi sat with me and comforted me in her arms.

"Yea. Thank you so much."

I felt alone with Jimmy's departure. It was silently calm. So, I did what most newly single twenty-two-year old's do. I bought a huge quart pot, vegetables, and learned how to can home made soup. I lasted a month apart from him, and he ended up moving back in. I couldn't call my sister again for help the next time. I thought they would be mad at me if they knew we were back together. I guess I had to keep him a secret now.

I could bet the next trip was going to cost me. I just hoped I would not have to pay with my life. One would think I was enthralled by pain. It might be blood, sweat, and tears, but for now, let's have a good time. I was up for a challenge and I forced the question: Can there be kindness in cruelty? I was a locked-up prisoner and a sucker for punishment. But the lilies were in bloom, and the weather was great in Saskatoon. We were going to see Good Riddance play live, and it was going to be a great show.

There were about a hundred and fifty people, and Jimmy left me sitting there with my drink. A few drinks later, he was still gone. He was annoyed at me because he was off "secretly" trying to find drugs. I had interrupted his mission. Through the opening and closing of the hall doors, I found him in the hallway where clanging noise vibrated all around. It was filled with kids having a great time, except for two. Forever grasping, but never holding.

I saw a feather that was floating in the wind. It appeared free. I did not know how it got there. It was dusted, with fine golden flakes. I admired its beauty with no remorse, and then looked back at my life.

"Hey, did you just see that?" one guy said loudly to his friends.

"That guy just pushed that girl!"

A group of guys started walking toward us, and Jimmy took off running. They chased after him into the parking lot. I ran after to see what was happening. Run, Jimmy, run! Oh no. They pulled him down to the concrete and ripped his brand-new white hoodie. His glasses went flying off.

"Don't ever touch a woman!" the one guy yelled as they circled around him.

After the siege was over, I asked him, "Are you okay?"

He was livid.

I picked him off the ground. Once again, it was all my fault. I should have never said anything to him about leaving me. Then none of this would have happened.

"Hey, are you going to stay with him?" Like I had a choice. I was not going to leave him stranded in the city. The stranger did not understand.

"I'm not leaving him here. He is my boyfriend."

"You're stupid," he said plainly and walked back inside.

The show was over. It was time to leave. As always, it came down to crashing blows. We got in the car and started to drive back home. The tension in the car had nowhere to go. We stopped at the convenience store. He bought a pizza sub and continued driving home.

The trees were tall ebony, a shade concealed against the night. The sky was black, like just before the lightning flashes and the temperature cools off. I sat still in the passenger seat, nervous. Jimmy was a mess. The darkest hour was upon us. He was still rambling on. My mind and emotions were exhausted. I couldn't handle any more negativity. I blurted out, "I'm done. We are breaking up! I'm so sick of this!"

"Oh really?" said the madman. "Well if you are going to leave me, then we are both going to die!" He swerved into the oncoming traffic lane, pressing down on the gas. Everything flashed before my eyes, and he was in the driver's seat.

"No!" I screamed out, panicking for my life. This guy was crazy. "What are you doing? No! No no no no no, please. Don't! No. I didn't mean it! Please don't kill us. Please!"

He steered the car back into our lane. Truly he was deranged – enough to leave me lying in ruins. I could see the blowing chaff along the roadside. Please God, I trembled, let the empty fields settle down, any one of them could be my open grave. How could I get away from him? Raced through my shell-shocked mind.

I had rolled the dice again. I had placed my bets on him. It was a bet that I would lose every time.

"Jimmy, let me please drive my car. I don't want to die in a car accident tonight. And neither do you. It's my car. Please let me drive."

"Okay, you can drive."

He slowed down, pulling over onto the shoulder.

I unbuckled my seat belt and jumped out of the car, running as fast as I could. I run along the highway, not sure if I should make a sharp left, down into ditch, and book it into the field. The fields were rolling yellow, with long grain crops. My heart pounded in my chest, as I jetted with all my might. He could have my car. Take it, go. Just give me my life back. I had to escape. The sword came out of its sheath and it was in full pursuit. My stomach turned. I knew my body would soon be aching. He threw me down hard, and I cringed against the blows on my body. I was precious, and this sucked. My pleading was never heard. I could not get over the fear that trembled through my body.

"Get in the car and drive home!"

This was the love that was being allotted for my precious silk charms?

It was hard to go against the kicks, and the dirt tasted like dirt. It was possible for so many things to go accidentally wrong – like him accidentally snapping my neck. One mistake, one time, was all it would take. Before it came down to that "one day", I would be a stiff, wrapped up in a black garbage bag. I would be hidden in a trunk and thrown out into a random garbage landfill. His rage and fury would be my end.

I put myself back into the car. I was a traumatized mess. This was not the life I wanted. I was trapped with no escape. I was nothing more than a rag doll.

God, can you hear me? I think I'm in some sort of amazing trouble. This man throws me around while I'm still alive. I know you see all the things we both do. In my weakness, I looked up, and saw his fury. He was not the man I knew. Where could I escape?

I drove down the highway, feeling like a prisoner. I looked down. My favourite white fuzzy sweater wasn't so cuddly anymore; it was ripped and full of dirt stains and blood. I tried to keep in my tears. I hated my life. I tried not to think about how torn up my heart felt after being trampled on. I felt like I should be lying in a hospital bed. I needed a cold cloth on my pounding head. They should have hooked me up to an IV and pumped back the blood I kept losing from him ripping out my heart. I was in shock. I was devastated, but numb. He had lied to me. He had told me he would never hurt me again. I knew he was going to keep doing it over and over. He would throw me up against the wall and crash my car into the night. Those were his plans – his greatest dreams. I was looking to be set free. Oh, sweet peace, please come to me now. You used to fill my soul. How could I forget all the comfort you once gave me? I kept forgetting all the King's ways.

A little harder every day. I could not chase his demons away. I could love him and give him my all, but I can't change him. In fact, he would be the one to change me. His love hurt and that would make my heart.

I gave him years to fix the problem, to "get better", but he never did. Worse still, meth showed up in town. It was coming in-between us. I knew the destruction of meth. I would come against it full force to try to stop it. Jimmy was over at his friend's place, sitting with a glass pipe filled with dope. I tore in.

"What are you doing?" My eyes flashed lividly.

I wanted to kill drugs, and it was me against them. He looked up, shocked that I would stand up to him. I grabbed his pipe and confronted both of these monsters. Bitter winds and dirty tides changed the moment he stood up, and the fight was on.

"I swear I'm smashing this pipe!" I crushed glass with my bare hands.

"Give it back!" His friends stood clear. Jimmy struggled to grab what I took.

It was wall-to-wall combat, then we were out the front door, and fell down hard on the ground.

He took my hand. I had my fist clenched. He pried it open and took his dope back.

It was over. I walked back home, down the street the pavement stood still. A little gloomy with my head hung defeated. Mad at myself. None of the promises he made to me were ever true. I couldn't keep living like this. I thought, choking back tears.

I opened the door to my house and walked into the washroom. I turned on the light and looked in the mirror, appalled at what I saw. I was a mess. My face looked aghast, covered in blood and dirt. My mascara run down my cheeks, made me look a fright in terror. My tears were black, staining my battered heart.

"He is ruining me." I could see that clearly when I looked at the miserable girl in the mirror. No one should live like this. These occurrences happened too frequently. Too many times for me to keep overlooking. This was only getting worse.

I turned on the tap and water started flowing into the sink. I got a cloth and wet it down. Gently cleaning my face up, I looked again at my reflection, knowing this was a moment I would never forget as long as I lived. This was not right. I was devastatingly broken. I was so hurt. This moment stood alone, like many. The one I loved destroyed my in most being. I held onto this brutal love that annihilated my soul. I deserved a better life. A life he could not give. This was not the plan for my future. "You have to leave him," I said to that girl I saw in the mirror. I kept choking on more tears. That night I packed my Ford Tempo and got in. Driving away, I watched out the rear-view mirror.

Looking for long-stem daises to pick from an open field. I walked along and remembered a promise I had buried a long time ago. The road was grown over with weeds, and I had lost myself along the way. I wanted to go back to a time that I just didn't know anymore. What is good, what is right, what is true? Somehow these things didn't apply to me any more. I was stuck in the mud. I was less than dirt, and I remembered the dust from where I had come. I found a broken piece of pottery that held its owner's ashes, and I picked it up. I held hope. I started dancing because the ashes weren't mine. I was amazed that I could find something beautiful in something so broken.

FOUR

DANCIN'

Life had a way of checking me in, but I always found the nearest exit. I was sketchy. Hiding in washrooms or behind doors so I could lock myself up along with all my fears. My mind made a shift that I didn't notice at the time. It probably was another one of those gradual, self-inflicted wounds. I ignored my conscious. My guilt seems justified from the pain, and general mistakes I kept making. The darkness bore down. I was sleeping in a reality that was constantly bombarding me and moving on, without moving on at all.

My dad always said to me, "It is better to go through life wanting something you never got, than getting something you never wanted." And I questioned him.

"Well, is it better to have loved and lost than to never have loved at all?"

I guess it came down to a bag of sticks and hammers, pitchforks and haystacks, and a box of love letters. They all burn.

A devastated 23-year-old drove down to Calgary. I had a broken heart the entire drive. I looked out the window, passing by perfect-looking homes. The houses looked well built, but I wondered if the same kind of violence went on under those roofs like at mine.

Dallas was living in the city with her two boys, and it was easy to find her address. She nursed me back to health, as the women in my life often did. They delicately wrapped white bandages of gauze around my heart to hold the broken strings and fleshy pieces together. We hoped my heart would heal, even if all the parts were not quite sitting in the right place anymore.

There were other causes for concern. I lived in a place with bright lights and limitless pawnshops that crack heads kept thriving down on Seventeenth Avenue, S.E. in Forest Lawn. One look at those pawn shops, I knew they spelled out T-R-O-U-B-L-E. I spent most of my time thinking about Jimmy. I was consumed by the lie that "I missed him terribly."

I transferred my job status and worked at 7-Eleven. I got home from work and thought about the really good day I had. This felt like a new adventure. I could appreciate healthy excitement. It was a half hour drive to Dallas's place from work, and we got along splendidly. It was nice to be back in her company.

Dallas had married, had two wonderful boys, and settled down beautifully. I enjoyed the drive to work and the life all around me. I was not so closed in by the four walls and temper anymore. Maybe I didn't need Jimmy anymore. Maybe life had more to offer than trauma, I suggested to myself. I was bouncing back. You can want with all your heart for something to work out, that does not mean it will. But by the time I realized it, Jimmy was on his way.

Jimmy and I moved into a basement suite that suited our needs. The walls weren't decorated with rainbow-coloured wallpaper. It didn't have star clouds that glowed in the dark on a dimmer light switch or perfect harmony that slid up and down with the window treatments. We weren't cookie cut. Jimmy and I were starting over, but it felt like it was me against him. So what was the point? If he was going to be a jerk, then why did he come? I knew this was a dangerous idea. I'm such an idiot. He was so angry. I didn't know if he was coming off drugs, if he was high, or who he was anymore. He acted like an angry animal.

One night at work a couple came in. They walked around the store like they owned it. I was busy scrubbing the grill, trying to get the baked-on grease off. She was five feet five, brunette, and her eyes sparkled against the silkiness of her tanned complexion; she was gorgeous. He had spiked, jet-black hair, white skin like a vampire, and very green eyes. There was another guy with them; he had soft light-blue eyes and was very cute.

They were chatty with me and came in every night. Her name was Kayla, and her boyfriend was Tom. The other guy was Matty. Kayla lived in Forest Lawn, and the two guys had come down for the summer to party. They were moving back to New Brunswick in the fall. I introduced Jimmy, and we all clicked.

On Valentine's Day, we went down to the Warehouse for a rave party. I had been staying away from drugs. The idea of going out to a party sounded tempting. It was a "special" occasion, so I agreed to use, but only because it was Valentine's Day. I hoped we would have a good time, but the chances of that actually happening were slim.

Tom had a bunch of ecstasy pills that made me feel euphoric. The room was dark and airy, silver smoke lingered. The music was pounding, sending me into a deep trance. The vibration from the loud music coursed through my entire body. It seemed harmless to just want to dance all night, but it progressed into everyone wanting to touch each other because their senses were being wildly over-stimulated. Jimmy, as usual, was off looking for more drugs while I sat there, wrecked out of my mind. Kayla was with me and asking, "Where is Jimmy?"

"I don't know, probably off looking for more drugs," I said, laughing and rolling my eyes while pushing the tangled hair out of my face.

"I don't think Jimmy and you should date! I think you need to leave him. He is going to kill you!" Kayla yelled over the loud music.

In the short time we had known each other, she had witnessed his explosive, crazy temper. He was hard-core and violent.

"I know. But it is hard. I have been with him for a while. He just moved up here. I thought things we be different. But they are worse."

The strobe lights flashed around the room. Darkness lit the place.

"Well, I'm here for you. You don't need him. He is no good for you." She smiled and hugged me.

"Thanks Kayla." I knew she was right.

"Come on, lets go dancin."

Kayla grabbed me by the hand and took me right out onto the middle of the dance floor where everyone could see us. Somehow, this life seemed so alluring. It seemed free and made it easy to forget your troubles. This was fun.

"You are brave. How can you dance like that? I can't dance," I said shyly, covering my face with my hands for a second. This was a new feeling. I closed my eyes and let go to the music.

"Whoooo!" Kayla yelled out in her own euphoria. She was smiling, shaking her head and finger at me. She was swinging her hips and moving her hands up in the air. Her energy was electric. "You go, girl," she said to me, grabbing onto my hand.

"You're so enchanting," I said, watching her. Kayla knew it, and just smiled at me.

"See, we are sisters. You don't need Jimmy anymore."

She grabbed my hands and lifted them high in the air. That night, like many, we danced the night away. Hours passed before Jimmy finally showed up. By that time, I was sitting down on a leather sofa. A guy was sitting next to me. Jimmy was upset, but he was the one who had taken off, not me. The night was over. It was time to go. I knew it would end like this. My friends and I all piled in the car.

On the drive home, the tension was building. I could feel thick negative energy. He did not say a word, and that was the warning. The ghost ship was cutting through rough waters, coming back around in the night. You might not hear the wind pushing against the sails, but it still keeps rushing silently. I was tired of shipwrecks, torn masses, and holes in the port, bow, and stern. At this point in time, Jimmy was not ready to love, nurture, or bring out the best in me, and vice versa. If I stayed, I was just a prisoner, tied to a chair, with heavy ropes in a gloomy dungeon from which I could not escape. My body was tired of being abused. It hurt. I needed help to get out before it was too late. I looked over my shoulder and into Kayla's caring eyes. The waves might crash, but it was safer overboard in black waters, and I decided I had enough. It was time to leave him.

Sitting in our basement suite on the couch.

"Are you sure you want us to leave?" Kayla and Tom asked.

It felt good to have support. Jimmy was in a state of madness. There was too much drama. And that is why I made this choice. "I need to stand up to him. I will come over after. Thank you guys."

My friends reluctantly went home. Jimmy was already freaking out and I found courage, "It is over. I am not going to be with you." He stared icily at me. Angered beyond the measure of his control. He grabbed me, threw me down on my head. It knocked me dizzy. I looked up at him, knowing I was defeated. He was aggravated, with stress lines permanently etched into his forehead. Another tell tale sign at a young age; he had endured severe emotional trauma and abuse. I knew it to be true, because I was starting to develop the same.

I hated this visitor, the monster. His wrath turned into a massive, life- threatening twister before my very eyes. He spun and spun out of control. I was paralyzed and filled with fear. I tried to shield myself from his destructive force. I cried out pleading to him, "please stop hurting me." He grabbed my arms and squeezed tightly. My eyes burned in pain from the tears. Fright was instilled into the deepest parts of me. He lifted me in the air and threw me around with trau-matic force; screaming at me, then pinned me down. He ripped off all my jewellery, one promise at a time. Finally, Jimmy got off me and left. I was wrecked. I sat on the floor curled up in a little ball, rocking myself back and forth; completely disabled.

A month later when my jewellery landed in the pawn shop, I phoned the police and pressed charges. District 4 came to the rescue. I invited them into my home and filed a report. After a couple hours, they took me down to the pawn shop and helped me get all my jewellery back. The police walked into the pawn shop and asked me, "Which rings are yours?"

I looked in the glass and pointed out, "that one, that, and that one." The police talked to the store owner and got the rings out. We went back out to the police cruiser where they gave me all my rings back.

"It is a rough neighbourhood." they gently warned, "allot of drugs and dangerous people. Be careful."

They were right. It was time for me to grow up and get on with my life. I distanced myself from the new friends. I used all my will power to get through the day. After a few weeks, surely things would get better. It was a constant emotional battle. I had sunken down low, stuck in the trenches. This is what I was up against: my abuser may be gone but living in the shadow of darkness did the same job. It held me down. *My place felt so empty, I had no peace, I was isolated, lonely, and miserable; those thoughts were lies.* It is called *oppression.* I needed peace, Jesus Christ, and His light to set me free. Praise God. There was hope, but I was still so blind.

It was an irrational and split decision. I gave into the temptation and I went back to my friends to start using drugs. Evil is possessiveness and it isolates to create the animal. I needed to protect myself from ever getting hurt again. The fear in me got to work. I needed to start building high, concrete walls and reinforce them with re-bar. They would be impenetrable. No one was going to ever get in or out. I did not realize how trapped I would become. I never realized I could lose my ability to be human. I was blind to the fact these choices rendered my soul dead. Drugs are a massive case of deception. Yes, they take it all away; even life itself. No love, people, family, or humanity. The plan was simple. First, I would get over Jimmy. Then I would get off drugs. It sounded logical to me, and I put it into action.

There is no truth in the devil. When he speaks a lie, he speaks from his own resources, for he is a liar and the father of it. John 8:44

I got high on "Special K," (which is a tranquilizer the vet uses to put animals down). I couldn't feel my legs, and I lost my balance completely. I couldn't stand up without tipping over. Only my mind left the sights and sounds of reality. I was in a washroom the entire time as I went on a journey, down into a K hole.

I was in a vast cave. It was huge and airy. I cautiously walked down a spiral staircase. It was carved out of rock that wrapped around the wall. I listened carefully for any sounds that I could make out, but all I could hear was a dripping noise that was not in sync and a strange echo. Was I safe in here? I came upon two gates with a bit of distance between them. The gates rested on the steps. They were iron and old. I opened one slowly. The gate squeaked loudly, it was creaky, as to alert my trespass, and I walked through.

I took slow, guarded steps forward. Where was I? This place was mysterious. Eventually I heard noise in the background. It sounded like carnival music playing. I came to an entrance. I asked myself, "Should I go in?" It looked like fun... it was a carnival after all.

I stood outside the entrance, detailing. I was mesmerized; the energy was alluring. The rides were wild. People filled the place with laughter. Wow, our town carnivals were lame compared to this place. Oh, this was off the charts with explosive entertainment. It looked harmless, so I walked in and wandered around.

The carousel ride was grand. The horses were gallant, beautiful steeds, decked out in colourful battle gear. Plus, there were rides that I had never seen before. I was enthused. It was clear that this place had it all. I was being swelled up in the mood. I felt on top of the world.

I noticed a clown sitting down in front of a striped tent. I had never seen a clown up close before. More excitement for me. The clown was sitting on a pail, and I gave him a great giant smile. He had big round circles on his cheeks, but wait – I was caught off guard! Woe. Under his paint he was washed-up looking. His eyes were sunken; black and evil with intense, miserable hatred. It was unexpected, and I backed away, bumping into someone. I quickly apologized and kept walking.

I noticed the people on the rides were staring at me. They were tragically gloomy. It was unsettling and suddenly, it felt awkward. It was becoming clear. I was a guest, and this was their home; they were stuck here. The people kept going around on the rides, but they were all miserable having to do so. That made me realize they could not leave. They were all pathetic prisoners, glaring right through me. Everyone here was dead. I was nervous to stay a moment longer. I needed to leave immediately.

I looked around – there had to be an exit. Keep calm, don't show that you are panicked. I abruptly picked up my pace. The music started changing; playing in slow motion. It became distorted. The atmosphere felt like it was turning upside down. The music, rides, and room all started to change the moment I realized I needed to escape. The timid slaves started disappearing one by one. They walked away, huddled over in terror. They were so brutally victimized; they dare not disobey their tyrant master. I could feel the oppression all around me. Whatever these people had suffered, it was unspeakable. Humans do not act like that.

The closer the master of deception got to me, the more distorted the music became. I took a quick look back and saw a shadow. It laughed. I look around frightened. The carnival was suddenly empty. It was dead silent. All the rides were stopped. The terrified hostages had disappeared. The level of fear in the room sky rocketed. I took off running! I looked back and saw what stood behind me. The presence of evil was happy to see me; it was the Joker.

I was horrified and screamed at the top of my lungs! I was in the room with the devil! No matter where I ran, I could not disappear like everyone else had. He was toying with me; he was the cat, and I was the mouse – until I ran hard right into his pronounced chest; and stopped dead in my tracks. I looked up, and he looked down upon me, wanting to devour me. He loathed me! He wanted me to see him! To fear him! Why else was he standing right there? Why, why, why? I looked up at him! His dark black eyes glared right through me. He had a hard, white plastic mask over his face. I couldn't see his face, and I didn't think to pull it off. The evil might have been so grotesque that I would never recover.

I was standing face-to-face with the very existence of evil. He stood in front of me, with his chest puffed out, and it heaved heavy as he breathed. He was an animal. What I sensed was something very primal. I stood there screaming in his face at the top of my lungs. I was terrified and took off. I had to get out of this place! This was the devil's playground! I was in his lair! What if I could never leave?

I was hysterical, and then I resurfaced back into reality for a moment, screaming in horror from the gruelling siege. I was back in the washroom and on the floor with someone who was holding onto me the entire time. "No! I don't want to go back!" I screamed in fear. Then I went back under again.

I was in the circus again, the freak show. I looked around, the people were on the rides, everything in the place was carrying on as if nothing happened. Again, I left the carnival, came back to reality, and stayed up. The drugs had worn off. I was exhausted. I went straight home and crashed.

I woke up the next day. My head was in a dark fog. So many wrong choices I continued to make.

High with Kayla, she pulled me into the washroom and locked the door.

"Sit down." she told me.

I sat down on the edge of the bath tub. She jumped up on the vanity.

"I am going to sing for you, okay." she said, smiling at me.

"Okay." I thought it was a bit strange, but she loved singing.

"Okay, let me think of a song. Um. How about Shakira?"

"Sure."

I did not realize I would be locked up the entire night, listening to every song that Shakira had ever sung. I concentrated. A few hours later, we left the washroom.

"Let's go for a drive." I suggested.

"Sure."

We drove around, it was daylight by that time. We approached the intersection and I stopped. I pressed on the gas, when a young girl smashed into us, head-on. No one was hurt in the accident, but it totalled my car. Months later, I received a large settlement of money. Thousands of dollars. Something that would last me a little while. I got a mountain bike instead of another vehicle. By the end of the month I am high using crystal meth. (I don't come down until I leave Calgary a few years later).

A few months after the summer had passed, school had started up for Kayla. Reminding me of her age. She was in Grade 12. She came over at my place. Earlier that week she had come back from New Brunswick. She had been visiting her boyfriend Tom and was feeling a little down from being away from him. We sat on the couch and talked.

"Hey chicky, how are you?" she asked.

I smiled at Kayla, "I'm doing good. How are you?" She was back in school, getting her life back on track.

"Oh, I'm good. School is okay I guess."

"How was your visit with Tom?" I asked enthused.

She sighed and dropped her shoulders, "it didn't work out with me and Tom."

I could see the disappointment in her eyes.

"Aww, I'm sorry to here that. Are you okay?"

"Ya, I love him and stuff. It sucks," she said, wiping a tear from her green eyes. "Well, maybe when I'm done school we will get back together. That is what Tom says."

"That is a good idea. So, you are still talking to him?"

"Ya, but not that much." she paused. Something was on her mind.

"I want to get high. Can we do some meth?"

I cringed within. I was dreading the moment she would ask me for crystal meth. I saw the question coming a mile away. I was prepared.

"I can't Kayla. I'm sorry."

"Please. I will be fine," she said, not knowing what she was asking from me. Absolutely I did not want this on my conscious. Me ruining her life.

"I was the exact same age as you when I first tried it. It ruined my graduation. I lost all my friends. Look at me now. Everything I held close I lost. It is so powerful, Kayla. I can't watch what it would do to you."

Kayla looked hurt

"It will strip you of everything."

"No, it won't. Please."

"I can't and I won't. I'm sorry. Trust me. I'm trying to help you."

When Kayla graduated, I was proud of her. It meant a lot to me. She could have the sweet, cherished memories of a grad night with her new boyfriend. A precious time of accomplishment and celebration.

I was thankful to have Kayla for a friend. She glowed. Her charisma oozed like a natural spring that lifts off the ground. We shared a lot of good times. She was often close by my side, looking after me. Kayla taught me how to dance a different way, how to be a hottie from head to toe, and how to have fun way past dawn. She was young; a vibrant beauty beyond her years. We built castles in the sky, forgetting all about boys and the broken hearts they cause. She strutted her stuff and loved showing it off. Yet, when I was with her, something inside wouldn't let me forget. I needed to watch for midnight because this all had to end. We were both all in, but somehow, I managed to slip out.

After many years passed, I checked in on her. I heard lots about her making beats and spinning at the club. Everyone noticed the enthusiastic, fun-loving girl who loved to go out dancin', dancin', dancin'.

When I heard the terrible news, I was gutted, and dropped to my knees. The news had been circulating on Facebook. They found Kayla dead.

"No." I don't want this to be.

I started opening all the old doors in my mind and walking through each one slowly and methodically. What was in here? Emotions that I had blocked off and feelings I had tried to kill. The room was dingy, filled with dense cobwebs. The dust was a thick layer that had settled on-top of old heavy blankets that covered my things. The room felt eerie and haunted. I noticed a single chair. I slowly walked around the room. My foot caught, and I almost tripped over a pile of ropes that were left forgotten on the old floorboards. This room was my old ghost ship. Kayla had met me here. I had been tied up in this room. I had been filled with fear. She had come up to me as I sat on the chair, and she started cutting the ropes loose for me. She said, "Girlfriend... it is time to leave."

I picked up the rope, examining it. It felt coarse against my delicate fingers. Once it had been tightly bound around my wrists. I remembered how Kayla helped me sever the knot. I held the rope in my hands and started to cry. I was free, and she was lost. A pigeon suddenly swooped in. I noticed the hole in the corner that it had flown in from. It had been my only escape. I remembered how she boosted me up and promised, "I'm right behind you!" And she was.

Kayla loved singing, dancing, and modelling. She loved music, laughing, and throwing her head back in complete, effortless beauty. She loved love, people, and she made everyone around her feel incredibly special.

Drugs stole her.

Dearest, sweet Kayla, I'm so sorry.

It crushes me that you never made it out.

It is quiet here.

And I will always remember you...

dancin', dancin', dancin'.

FIVE

THE HOLIDAYS

Trapped and buried alive. The seal held up, and no one had been able to get into the hellish room where I lived. Tidal waves from natural disasters crashed against the walls that came tumbling down. In this dark bottomless pit, I breathed death with every heartbeat. My lease on life changed as every day passed. I had no use for flashy strobe lights or anything that blinked. With every hit of the pipe, a new day dawned, and I was numb. My loss was buried with me. I had strength and pride beyond anything human. I dared anything to try and come in the way of my "freedom". It was not going to happen. My brain felt as though it was shutting down from jolts of electricity and stringing up anything that wanted to hang. Boys, I was done. I wanted nothing that life had to offer, except out. I wanted three things: pedal bikes, hair wigs to hide my identity so I wouldn't get caught selling, and enough dope to never run out. That was enough for people to show up and buy drugs from me.

One night, two guys I had sold to walked into my room. One pulled out a butterfly knife and started twisting it around, playing with it in front of me. I looked back at him, as if he had the problem, not me, and I looked away. I didn't know what his problem was. They both were tall, had dark hair. One was husky and the other lean. I talked to the guy who I had sold the drugs to, not the one with the knife.

"What was the problem?" I asked, standing as far across the room as I could get.

"You ripped us off."

"What? No, I never."

"Yes you did!"

"How? You didn't get high?"

"No!" he retorted.

"Well. How did you do it?"

"We put it in the pipe, and it turned all black. It didn't melt! It wasn't meth."

And they confirmed everything I thought.

"I told you it was K. There is no meth around. I told you that six times."

I was relieved when they left. I needed to change my locks and get better reinforcements.

I did rip someone off, but only once. His name was Avery. Ave was in his forties, and I barely knew him. From what I saw, he liked having a good time. It always begins as something "harmless". He was not out to hurt anyone. He bought lots of drugs off other people. I sold to him here and there, but his paper was burning up fast. I heard he had been a professional athlete – a race car driver – and had a bad accident. Somehow, he got hooked on painkillers, and it progressed to crack or anything he could get his hands on.

I went over to his place one evening, and he met me at the door with a friendly smile, welcoming me in. I walked into his place like so many other times before. It always felt gloomy and smelled like crack cocaine. Inside his apartment, he was all over the place and sketched out. I could see he was upstairs living in a mind that was rattled, electrically charged, and over-stimulated from short fuses.

"I need a cuff. I will pay you back double if you help me out, please, I'm good for it. Please, please," he said with his hands together. I was surprised.

"Uh, don't ask so much man – it's all good. Get up. Of course I will help you."

I opened a vial of "Special K" that was around my neck and dumped a pile of dope on a plate.

"Merry Christmas!" I said cheery eyed, giving him the best gift I could give a fellow addict. "Thank you!" he said jumping around. "I love you! Thank you!"

His hands were waving in the air. He was ecstatic. Whatever he was going through, I wanted the best for him. And I smiled at him.

It felt so lonely in his place. The silence was screaming and darkness rested on the mantle. Where winter fires should be burning, children's stockings hung, and laughter shared, just felt dead. In this apartment, Christmas felt like gloomy shadows that came upon the whole room with lies and emptiness. What remained was the sense of finality. He was broken. It was a matter of hours before his clock would finish counting down.

Ave walked me to the door. I felt the need to try and encourage him somehow. I wanted to tell him that he was important and special, and that he was not alone, like he probably felt at the time.

"I like you. You're a good guy and you deserve to be happy," I said to him. He was staying at home for Christmas, all by himself. He had lost his career, friends, family, purpose, and connection to the outside world – his humanity. He was stuck in the pit he had dug himself, and I was standing there, looking down over the edge. He was holding on by a final string. Looking up at me, he said goodbye.

"I like you too, and I think you're a good person. Merry Christmas," he said back, giving me a boyish smirk. I looked in his lost brown eyes. They were intensely sunken, and the moment gripped me. His broken eyes took me into hollow depths of utter hopelessness. I stood at his door, not moving or wanting to leave him at all. Ave faced me, and I was worried by what I saw. By giving him the one thing I thought would help him, I left him with the one thing that would help take him away.

I never noticed my raver friend Tdo walking up to us. Tdo was there to walk me to work, so I left with him. Tdo was short, had brown hair, and blue eyes.

"Bye."

"Bye." And Ave shut the door.

I walked away, shook to my core.

"Hey Tdo, I got a bad feeling about Ave here. He is troubled. I don't think he is going to make it. Will you please come back and check up on him?"

Tdo chuckled light- hearted. "Oh, Ave is fine."

"No. I don't think so. Please just check on him. It will make me feel better."

"All right. Fine."

"Promise me?" I said seriously.

"Yes. I promise."

"Thanks."

I walked to work for the night shift. It was a gorgeous evening. Light snow was tenderly falling in the silence of a quiet street. Not a creature was stirring. The blanket of snow was soft, it seemed so pure against the abstract of my life. I passed the payphone outside my work, picturing how Ave used it many times a day.

After work, Dallas was waiting to take us back home to my parent's place. I left for Christmas, bringing my own holiday cheer. My entire family was all there. Mother put on a lovely meal; mashed potato's, gravy, stuffing, ham; the food went on for days. The table spread was festive with candle light. Yummy fruit punch that tasted sweet and fizzy. My favourite was the frozen pistachio dessert. By the end of the meal we were all way too stuffed to eat another bite.

My sisters glanced at one another, and my parents sat across the table, sharing their own looks. I felt out of place and wondered how everything was going back home. Maybe it was that year we discovered the fire place channel. It filled up the room with as much artificial heat as a fan can flame. I smiled at the children, while feeling like the worst aunt alive. I detached myself from any meaningful conversations. I was not anyone my family knew. And I went back home a week later.

I was at work when a lady came into the store and started talking to me.

"Did you hear what happened to that guy in apartment 29? I think you were friends with him."

"Um, no. I did not hear anything."

"They found him dead. He was hanging in his apartment."

This was beyond anything I could process.

"No way." My heart dropped. "What? Are you serious? How did they find out he was dead?"

"The smell that was coming from his place. I guess the manager had to go in and found him in the living room."

"Oh no." I shook my head. I gasped. I was appalled. I did not know what to say.

The lady left the store, and I went to the back room to be alone. I couldn't believe it was true. But it was.

I went home from work and took all my "Special K" and flushed it down the toilet.

"Never again!" I swore to myself.

There are no words to describe what happened in Ave's apartment. It happened over fifteen years ago, but I still replay it over in my head, as if it were yesterday. I will never forget the look of suicide in Ave's eyes, and how I turned and walked away. I sat on my couch crying. Looking over the final moments of a forever goodbye. His eyes, his smile, his pain and wounds. His thoughts. His defeat. His place. His final decision. I wondered if God would ever be able to forgive me? Could I ever forgive myself?

SIX

JOY IS GONE

I also experienced suicidal thoughts. You get high. Trip out. Some nights, for whatever reason, evil comes to torment you and the idea of peace looks brighter; the moon is a little fuller, and the temptation is so much nearer. Sometimes you have to fight your hardest to stay alive throughout the night. After a good sleep, you wake up, glad to still be alive. You realize darkness had visited you and was there to try and finish you off, once and for all.

After Ave passed, things really changed inside of me. I was even more guarded, super disconnected, mean and angry. I associated with very few people. I moved closer to Scott, a guy who lived in the basement where the walls around him whispered, "Keep your voice down." Scott was pale and looked similar to Eminem I thought. He wore a black bandana and obsessed about me all day long, writing rhymes constantly. He called me "No mercy Marci."

His room was clean. He had a stereo. On his dresser nightstand next to his bed were pencils and pens. There was panelling on his walls and a small window above his bed that people gently tapped on when they walked by to let him know they were there. The window was covered by a curtain that closed out all sense of time, life, or urgency.

"Hey Scott, how's it going?"

"I'm good Marci. How are you?"

"I'm good." I smiled.

"Are you hungry? Do you want me to go make you something to eat?"

"Awww. Sure!"

Scott made sure I ate and drank, or else I forgot.

I took off my coat and got comfortable while I waited for him to fly back in the room with a delicious peanut butter and jam sandwich. I smiled at Scott when he came back in.

"Thanks," I said as he kindly handed me a plate and sat down on his bed.

"I wrote another rhyme. Do you want to hear it?"

"Ya! Totally," I said enthused, and his eyes lit up.

"I mean it. I've seen it, been it, repeatedly defeated, the conceited..."

"Knock, knock, knock. Who you got over now Scott?"

It was Scott's grandpa. Scott jumped up quickly motioning to the door.

"Just Marci is here," he said. His grandpa looked in at me, and I gave him a smile, which was good enough for his grandpa, and then he turned around. Scott closed the door, distracted by the interruption.

"How about I put on some music?"

"Sure"

Scott went over and started flailing through his CD's.

"Okay, what do you want to listen to?"

"Whatever you want to listen to," I said, noticing his perfectly tied bandana.

"Uh, do you have any Hard house?"

"Um, I don't think so. Hey Marci, did you hear about Tdo?"

I stopped eating my sandwich for a second, thinking about the last time I talked to Tdo. I had not slept for a few days and had been tripping out about getting busted. I had taken off on my pedal bike in the dead of winter. I peddled with nowhere to go and eventually took a turn down 17th Avenue. I biked past a pawn shop and threw away all my drugs in a snow bank. I left them behind and didn't think twice about doing so. I had told Tdo where I had tossed them and had not seen him since. It had been a week or two, so I thought he probably went and found them.

"No, what is happening with him?"

"Well, he was high and cut off his nipples."

"What. Why? That is disgusting."

Scott shrugged at me, smiling.

"Oh, that is messed up. How? Why would he do that? Where was he?"

"With a razor blade. I'm not sure why. I guess he was at home in his basement. He is messed up. Guess what else, Marci?"

"I don't think I want to know, do I?"

Scott sat back, "Guess who I met?"

"Who?" I loaded up my pipe with a bowl to smoke.

"Jimmy."

"What? Woe." I instantly held my hand up, motioning him to stop everything.

"Where and how did you meet him? What did you think of him?" My chest tightened.

"He was with some friends of mine. I think you should stay away from him."

"Ya, I usually do, but I still kind of love him, ya know?"

"Ya, I do. I just don't know why."

Scott was right. What was once built had been forever destroyed. All the dope or money in the world could not buy a new heart. My heart was dead. Limp and lifeless.

"Let's smoke a bowl...thanks for the sandwich."

I had given Jimmy my heart long ago. What a waste of time that turned out to be. I never hated Jimmy. I missed him. I was afraid of what he would do to me the next time I saw him. The last time we were together, it was brutal. He had smashed a window to get into the house, and he had gone ballistic. After that, I picked up the pipe and never put it back down. No. I would never be hurt again. I would never be vulnerable again. Toxic to death and manic to die, where was life now? It was some hidden treasure that I did not have a map for. I was sure hell was breaking loose wherever he was. I was thankful I was "safe". I left Scott's house to go meet some people.

When it came to Jimmy, it seemed like the tables had turned. The view was much better from up here. I would not let him shake me down this time. I was ten feet tall. I thought I still loved him, but I would love him secretly. He always forced me to flee down dark paths to escape his terror.

Eventually, Jimmy showed up at my place. It should have felt like comfort in a world of strangers. He was an "old friend", and those are usually the best kind. You hold them to a higher standard because they are tried, tested, and proven to be true. But history always has a way of repeating, and in no time, I started feeling uncomfortable; like at any moment Jack the Ripper was going to jump out at me.

People were leaving my place. It was just him and me – a situation that was never safe. I was aware of where I was sitting in correlation with the door. I had my dope on me, and I was already wearing my shoes. My money was in my bag with my phone. All these things I needed with me for when I would have to make a break for it and run for my life. Okay, my bases were covered; now I had to watch his tone and body language to see how fast he got irritable. We sat facing one another. We weren't confessing any faults or trying to get clean; it was more like staring one another down before the bomb went off. It took less than an hour before he blew. He grabbed my propane bottle and lifted it up to push the ignition start.

"I'm going to start you on fire!"

CLEAVE TO JESUS CHRIST

I bolted out the door, not waiting to find out if he was serious or not.

"I'm going to light you up!"

I flew over to the Macs convenience store parking lot. Jimmy was holding my blowtorch and was right behind me. He was blitzed with madness! The Fiend in him was ready to kill the Fiend in me. It was a showdown.

"I'm going to light you on fire!" he taunted, threatening me with wild provocative eyes.

"Leave me alone!" I screamed hysterically, maybe somebody will do something. I have to freak out in the parking lot.

"Don't touch me!" I yelled at the top of my lungs.

People were walking by, watching everything that was going on. He lunged for my bag, but I fought for it! I wasn't backing down. I was strong, just as untamed or even more so than him.

I heard sirens approaching. It was as if I had been rescued from the hand of death. I was thankful beyond comprehension. I watched Jimmy take off and I took off too, sketched out.

My heart was pounding. I had never felt it beating so ferociously loud in my entire life. I keep up a fast pace walking down the sidewalk. It was about eleven at night. I was looking all around me. My mind zoomed. Was I safe from the certain destruction Jimmy caused? Right then, I cried out and thanked God. It was God's hand that protected me.

The police came around the corner and pulled up.

"Are you the girl who was involved in the confrontation in front of the Macs?"

"Yes," I nodded, blitzed out of my gorge.

"Where are you going? We need to talk to you."

"I'm going home."

"Where is the guy who was after you? Is he there?"

"I have no idea. He may be there. It's 210 Fonda Court... in the basement."

"Okay, meet us there."

I nodded.

I had been so consumed with the dope I had in my bag. It was weighed out and packaged individually. I was fixated on that. I completely forgot about the conditions of my basement suite. I lived in a tweaker's paradise. It did not cross my mind I had just told the police where I lived, inviting them into my home – Satan's den. The force of demonic activity was at an all-time high; and I was blind to the actual depths. I looked around for a place to stash my dope. I was sinking fast. As I got closer the cop came outside. He was waiting for me. Great.

I walked into my apartment. Jimmy was sitting on my couch. His eyes were glued to me. He was tripping out as bad as me. Why do I never learn? I wished I had nothing to do with him. This was all his fault – the constant drama, non-stop, and all the problems that he got us into. It made me hate him all over again.

The police were gasping, looking around shocked. Had they never seen a drug addict's house before? It seemed normal to me to have scales, broken glass and pipes, glass test tubes, and blow torches lying around the room. Really all the paraphernalia one could imagine. I wasn't living at home anymore and baking muffins for the commonwealth. I could do whatever I wanted. The place was filled with bikes that had been taken apart, bongs, and graffiti-drawn sketch pictures from my friend Matt on the walls. My place was a mess. No. No normal person lived here. I couldn't tell the police that Jimmy was trying to light me on fire. I could see it in his eyes: "If I go down, you're going down with me."

Finally, all my choices were catching up with me. Consequences were serving out a sentence. I just never thought it would be me. I was never that "bad" person. Tonight was unravelling like wallpaper, and I couldn't get a handle on it. The design was already on the paper. This was the choice I had decided to decorate with. All I had to do was wet the paper and stick it up on my walls. I never saw myself being up for the task, but I went ahead away. Selling drugs was just something I had gotten caught up in. My mind raced in utter panic as the cops looked through my things. Who knows what else they would find.

"Um, I think I need help," I confessed, with my head lowered, shaking it in disgust. "I'm addicted to drugs, and I can't quit."

"Where are your parents? Do they know?" The woman cop asked with serious concern. The cops could see I lived in a home that was completely demonic. They could see it the second they had walked in. Satan was over every inch of my place. I lived in devil's dust and tombs. And I just thought I was an addict. No. It was much deeper then anything I would ever be willing to admit to.

"My parents live in Drayton Valley. It is about three hours away." I kept crying. I made sure to drown out the shock of the other officer, who was rummaging through my things in the other room. I pretend to not pay any attention to anything other than the huge need I had for help. Clearly my life was immersed in drugs... it's not like I could hide it. I might as well own it and go for an Emmy with this performance.

Oh, wickedness lived festering in my bones. It was crafted like thick ornamental cartilage that rung in my ears and wore me out around my fingers. I needed a huge long syringe to puncture the bone marrow in my back and come out with some density; and a plan to discontinue all further experimentation's on how many ways I can get high.

"No, I don't think my parents know. But if they did, they would help me," I said confidently.

"Well what about this guy? Wasn't he chasing you with a blowtorch?" the cop questioned me.

I looked to Jimmy who looked at me. He was not saying a word, and I sobbed even more.

"Uh, oh no... I don't even know what that was all about... no, he would never hurt me."

My tears were flooding down, and I let the current sweep me into the washroom to blow my nose and stash my bag with all my drugs under the bathroom sink.

"What's your name?" they asked Jimmy.

"Mike Polanski," Jimmy answered, giving them a fake name.

"Do you have an ID?" the man cop asked.

"No, not on me. I don't have a wallet."

I came back out of the washroom after I had composed myself.

"Will you call your mom and tell her the trouble you are in?"

"Yes, of course."

I was so relieved and thankful to God.

"Thank you," I told both officers.

They left.

Jimmy and I were stunned, both totally speechless.

One minute I thought the tables had turned, but the next, I was at his mercy again. You can plan for company, clean your house, do the dishes, get food ready, and make sure everything is proper. You never can quite plan for when the police show up at your door. Then you are undressed, your hair is a mess, and all they see is fighting. A day of disaster. You don't really plan for disasters either, unless you realize that's what your whole life has become; and then I guess you should expect it. Jimmy and I were over. It didn't hurt like I had told myself it did. The pain was gone. I could always love him, but I finally accepted that I was making it on my own, and I was safer and better off without him.

I woke up the next day thankful about the close call the night before. I had received a major free pass on that one. Just another day. I rolled over to hit a packed bowl. Evil filled my entire body. My brain felt fuzzy as if it was short-circuiting. My eye sight was becoming weak, and my vision was a touch blurry from the constant strain I put on my eyes. The room was filled with thick smoke that I could cut with a knife. Before my feet touched the ground, I was wrecked and getting ready for my day. I forget those closest to me. The ones I loved were just distant memories now.

I heard a "knock" on my door and went to answer it, ripped out of my mind! The smile was instantly slapped off my face. To my horror, it was my family, standing at my door. Without hesitation, I slammed the door in their face, locked it, and hustled to my bedroom. I was tripping out.

You need to get out of here!

I grabbed my power drill.

You can't let them take me away from you!

I was not going to let my parents see me or my place, like this. I started unscrewing the bars off my windows. My mind surged. I had to get out of there. What in the world were they doing here? They would see my place. I would be so busted, not to mention completely ashamed! They would take me away from it all. I just knew it.

They can not be trusted; they are the enemy!

I could hear them knocking at my door.

"Joy, please let us in. We want to see you."

Ya right.

It had been me and the darkness for so long. It would never give me up.

You don't want to go through all that pain again, do you? It will be even worse than before. You will be so lonely. You won't be able to stand it.

I never wanted to be vulnerable or ever have feelings ever again. It hurt so much. All the love I had searched for was twisted and jaded black. If I were to give up dope, it would mean a world of pain waiting for me. The past was never far. I was always dragging it around with a luggage strap from room to room inside my head and heart. I had managed to close off and seal off all the doors and then stack brick and mortar in front, just to be sure no one could get past. No one was crossing over the line. So, when my family came knocking and caught me off guard, they couldn't expect a welcome. They could not come in my world. They did not belong in it. I did not have time to fake being fine, and I couldn't even try. I had turned into monster.

The drill could not work fast enough. Hyperventilating admits the imprisonment of fear. I had spent so much time installing bars on my window for safety, and now I had to rip them off. I got the bars off and hoisted myself out. The daylight was blinding to my hurting eyes, and I ran as fast as I could. I left them standing at my door. The element of surprise did not help this situation. My family was there to fight for me, but I was so caught. I had no time to hide behind my mask the devil had given me on a different date and time. I had not even remotely realized how much the devil had taught me, I confidently conceded. Joy was gone.

I ran over to Scott's place.

"Scott! My parents are here! Like, they just surprised me, and I took off. What do I do?"

"Woe, they are at your place?"

"Mmmhm."

"Well call them. See where they are, and what they want."

I had not thought of that in my panic. I dialed them up with my heart pounding.

"Hello?" Remi's sisterly voice picked up.

"Hi," I said cautiously. "What you doing?"

"We are having supper at the restaurant. It is actually right down the street from your place. Have you ever been there?"

"Um, like no. I haven't," I replied cautiously.

"It's really nice. You should come join us, if you want. We would love to see you."

"Really?"

Why are they being so nice? I scratched my head. This was way too suspicious.

To my surprise, they were calm, like nothing had happened. I had their forgiveness without even asking for it? Strange. I could always count on Remi to be the brains of any successful combat mission. She had cast out the hook, but would I take the bait? Just the fact that they were there said they cared. Remi and Mom were constantly trying to help build me up. They had put so much of themselves into me. Time after time, my family had been there, picking up after my mistakes and sweeping them onto a great big pile. Once gathered, they threw them all away in the garbage for me with thoughtfulness. I never stopped to realize the work or pain I often caused. And this was my thanks to all of them. I had spent a lifetime of making memories, and to think, I couldn't just reach deep down and grab onto something that remained good inside of me, or to find some saving grace. I didn't know when they had lined up the visit to come see me. Most likely it had something to do with the police from the night before. There was no how-to book on how to save your kid from crystal meth. I was desperate for help, and it was looking bleaker each moment that they sat there waiting for me to show up.

"Well, how about we give her another half hour?"

"Okay."

Remi looked at Mom, Dad, and Ken, who sat facing the door to the restaurant with hopeful expectations.

"Okay, how about another fifteen? If she doesn't show, we will go."

"Sounds good."

Tick. Tick,

"Well, just ten more."

The family was sitting around the table having a conversation about how to handle me when I showed up, and what not to say.

Tick. Tick. Tick.

Finally, the entrance door to the restaurant opened up and the sun shone in. It was like a sign of hope. Everyone around the table was nervously looking at one other.

"This is it. Tread carefully," my parents warned, "this may be our only shot."

Ken's blue eyes and gorgeous grin looked up at the girl making her way to the table.

He gently leaned in and whispered, "It's not her." The light in my parent's eyes was sucked out, and they felt gut-wrenching despair.

Across town, I was sitting on a chair in a pitch-black room. I was helplessly summoned and obedient to the night.

She made it sound too easy. You can't trust them. You're not safe to go anywhere near them!

I was consumed by fear. It clung to me, so I never showed. I felt horrible and like the worst person alive for not making it to that restaurant. I was surprised that I could actually blow them off. It showed how disconnected and cold I truly had become. I felt huge guilt.

I had built a shrine of deceit that was sinking me into a smoke-filled hole. Illuminated eyes were glowing all around me. Watching me, I watched them. No one ever blinked. Surprises kept coming. What could I expect next? This lunacy was charming me. It had a way of keeping me in the fold. I didn't trust anyone. I constantly kept changing the locks on my doors, just in case. I was so confused. I had so many deadbolts with too many keys that I couldn't keep straight. I had too many masters.

Months passed. Who knows? The timeline was lost on me, maybe it was years. The feeling came over me suddenly. No sounds or warning signs. No fog or icy patches. Just time and regret.

I sat on my bed thinking about my grandma. If she could see my life and how I had turned out... I had not planned for my life to go so desperately wrong. Does anyone?

The oppression lifted for a moment, and I felt human again. I would give anything to go back. I was supposed to love Jesus, like her. This was not the life I wanted. I remembered the smell of her house, the lime green carpet in her living room, and all the times I had spent there. I was told Grandma had been born with a hole in her heart. It had given her trouble over the years. I just figured that was why she was so full of love and the reason she cared so much.

I started writing her a letter. For so long I had justified all my actions in a twisted way that made sense to a person living in sin. But I came face to face with the truth when I started writing my grandma to apologize. The words I spoke came from a broken soul. The words were too dark to send, but I needed to get them out. I was far away with wounds that needed healing and asking for forgiveness seemed like the right place to start.

The wellspring of my life breached, and this time, I welcomed the pain. I cried with every word I wrote. I told Grandma how much I loved her and what she meant to me. The ink was blue, but it smudged when my tears dropped down on the paper. Every part within me needed watering, and maybe it would be enough to grow this promise directly to her.

"Grandma, I'm sorry. I know my life is a mess right now. You have seen me going downhill. I have let you down. I promise you, with all my heart, I will make it. I will see you in heaven..."

Drenched with tears, finally I was being held. It was a seamless extraction from cords of love bound to me. I got an envelope and tucked the letter inside, sealed it, but I never sent it.

A month later she passed away. She was home. She lived for the glory of Jesus. I knew she would be watching down on me.

It was time I stopped using and I was not planning to blow it. My life depended on it. I definitely wanted to spare my grandma from seeing me above.

SEVEN

BOYS MY DAD
WARNED ME ABOUT

I thought about Grandma. How happy she must be with Jesus and how shameful my life was. I was certain she had seen it all now. There was nothing I could hide. All my plans for sobriety looked like they were passing me by. I felt completely lost.

Riffraff of a new crowd kept showing up at my door. Whether I opened the door or not, they still were pounding it down to find a way in. My life was in constant danger; I just didn't realize how much.

I was in my one-room apartment and working on my bike. That is when Blare just showed up, uninvited. I did not trust Blare's black eyes. I saw the vacancy within them, they did not quite match my own. I trusted no one. I wanted to be left alone. I was afraid of anything that moved. The anxiety I felt was incredulous. The situation at my tweaker's pad was out of sorts. Between the darkness of slithering snakes, and the shame that crawled on my floors, there was no reality. I was completely broken, down to the pulp. People and life did not exist in my residence. And I never noticed. I only feared more of it coming in. A village of eyes hid in the bushes outside of my home. The helicopters flew above my room in the early dawn hours. And there was someone always watching. Waiting for me to come bring them drugs. I guess using drugs to get over Jimmy had not really gone as I planned. This existence devoured me, leaving no room for escape. It was a winding road that led only to one's death. The fun party times were short lived. Now it was a constant nightmare of evil.

"Hey, I brought someone to meet you," Blare said, perma-sketched out. His dark hair was messy, and in that heart lurked something deeper that I did not trust. It meant serious trouble for me. Not to mention, a few months' prior, his ex-girlfriend threw a cup at him from across the room. It hit him in the head and knocked him off kilter, causing permanent brain damage.

"No. Uh. I don't want to meet anyone! Don't bring anyone here!" I said looking at him nervously. No strangers needed to know where I lived. The last thing I did was tell anyone where I lived. People kill for drugs.

There was light tap on my door as Blare retorted, "Well it's too late."

A tall guy strutted into my place like he planned to own it. I summed him up instantly. I was threatened by the personification he projected. I did not trust that perfect smile. I could see in those jet-black eyes was hatred. His charm could not cover the wicked that he planned to unleash.

He wore all black; a leather jacket that was as sharp as the night, except for bright white shoes. He had black, spiked hair. His name was Drades.

In no time, Drades started showing up at my place. He demanded to know who I knew, where I was going, and all the details of my private life. I stayed away from gambling, unlike him. Any money he made he gambled away, and by the end of the night he had nothing left, except a wicked plan.

Early in the morning, I left my place at 4:00 a.m. to run some dope. I raced the traffic with my Kona Kula bike. I soared along the early heights that dawn. I was comatose behind my force field – pink Ryder sunglasses. It was a perfect spring morning. Thrill was in the air. It felt as if there was no trouble in sight. I had anticipated my stop at the Macs to pick up a Slurpee and some five-cent candy.

I waited for the fire trucks to pass me on the highway before I crossed the road. Their loud sirens were blaring so loud that I had to cover my ears. That alarm would wake anyone up. I went into the Macs and got my breakfast. I walked my bike back the rest of the way to my basement suite. I was so lost in the moment of pleasure. Oh, those candies were so good! I was enjoying them immensely! I just loved their Slurpee's as well; they were the right consistency at any hour. The candies were so chewy and delicious! Me and candy. Yum, yum, it was a great way to start a new day. It made me so happy.

I walked around the corner. I could smell a fire blazing. Smoke was rising from a neighbouring house. Oh no. My heart went out to them right away. It was so early in the morning. Someone must have left a cigarette burning or something. Thick smoke was billowing up. That is too bad, I thought as I kept walking along. Wow, what a close call. That fire sure was close to my place. People were coming out of the building coughing. Hey, wait a minute. I stopped and took a closer look. I know those people...oh no. It is my place. This must be all my fault. I instantly blamed myself and asked how I could have been so careless. Not to mention, my poor neighbours were going to hate me; I burned their home down. Plus, I was going to be homeless. I cringed. I stood around with my neighbours watching the fire helplessly, feeling their glares penetrating through me.

Finally, I go into my place. The smell of smoke and ash feeding off my home was all I could taste. The walls had turned grey from all the smoke. I was thankful that it was not worse than what it was. My couch, living room, and kitchen were congested with smoke.

I walked into my bedroom. This is where the fire had started. My things were burned, and the room was covered with soot. It was a grim scene and looked as if a reaper had ravaged my place. I looked around the room. It felt eerie, as if the fire was trying to speak to me, and as if it had a personality of its own, trying to tell me what exactly happened.

I had a huge sliding closet mirror door that I had hung horizontally across my bedroom wall. It was smashed! My heart sunk further. A green propane bottle was left there, under the mirror, it was lying on the ground. Someone had thrown that bottle hard, while it was lit, and tried to blow up my apartment.

"Who did this?" I felt so much animosity towards me. Someone hated me intensely. I was stunned. I stood there, shaking my head. Someone was stalking me. Why would someone want to purposely hurt me? I looked around my room. It was a feeling I had never felt before. I started looking through my things to see what had burned. An investigator came in and started asking me some questions.

"Who would do this to you?"

Clearly it was Drades, but lately anyone was suspect. Since knowing Drades, he had broken into my place, stolen over a thousand dollars, robbed over an ounce of my dope, smashed my cell phone, held me hostage, and now he had lit my place on fire. Losing my life over selling drugs was not worth it to me. I was not ready to die as a messed-up drug addict who was headed straight for hell. I needed to move quickly. I packed up my lonely and moved out at the end of the month.

EIGHT
NO BRAKES

I settled in my new place feeling safer. I was in a one-bedroom basement suite and the walls were a peachy colour. The place was another death trap of walls and a furnace that was lit up. I was out all night, biking around the city. I was exhausted by the time I got home. I sat down on my couch and it melded me into it. I was beyond exhausted. "I need to lock the door." I remind myself, and instantly crashed. Zzzzzzzzzzzzzzz.

I woke up the next day confused.

The door was standing wide open.

Oh no. Who came in my place?

I jumped down off my couch to close the door and my pants fell off. Someone undid them.

I pulled them back up, and now I needed to check my bag. Great. It was empty. I had enough.

I had been robbed again. It was time to call the police and file a report. I needed some protection here. Selling drugs was really getting to me. If they could investigate this intrusion for me I would be so thankful. I had a shower. Then I phoned District 4 police and waited.

"Knock, knock."

I hopped off the couch and answered the door.

It was Ana. She had been my friend for a while now. She had blue eyes and long, cornrow-braided hair under a beanie hat. She lived downtown. She came in and gave me a suspicious smirk, which showed her piercing that was inside the front of her mouth.

"Hey, Ana, how's it going?"

She shrugged her shoulders and carried her blue BMX bike inside. "Good," she said, giving me sketchy side eyes.

"How are you?"

"Not good dude. Like I got jacked. I got nothing."

"Dude are you serious? Like what happened?"

"When I woke up today the stuff in my bag was gone, and the door was wide open. I'm pissed. I called the cops and have been waiting for like, three hours now."

"Well like do you think it's your neighbours?"

"Um, like I think it might be."

Ana sat there for a moment, looking around my place. She was looking up at the registers on the ceiling.

"Dude what if the people upstairs put like some kind of chemical down your vents, that like knocked you out?"

I looked at her. That was utterly ridiculous.

"No, like dude, I don't..."

"Knock, knock."

"Oh, that's them..."

I jumped off the couch and answered the door. Two good-looking young cops were standing there.

"Come in."

The cops come in and stood in the middle of the room. They looked around casually before asking, "What can we do for you?"

"I wanna file a report. In case I don't have enough rent money. I want it on record that I was robbed. I got home early, and I shut my door. I fell asleep right there over on that couch. When I woke up, the door was open, and my rent money was stolen out of my bag."

"Who do you think did it?"

"Um, maybe my neighbour?" I guessed.

"Which one?" The cops asked, looking at one another.

"Well," Ana piped up, "I think it could be her neighbours that like, live upstairs." She started pointing to the registers on the ceiling. "I think they are like putting poison down her vents to knock her out."

"No, actually I don't think so." I said to them, interrupting her.

They laughed, "Well, there is nothing we can do for you."

"What? You can't do anything? Are you serious?" I was utterly shocked.

Their humour about the situation made me regret calling them at all.

"Lock your door next time, okay?"

I jumped off my couch to let them out. I was pissed. Ana was livid. "I can't believe they didn't do anything! Cops are like, supposed to help, and like, they didn't do anything! You could have been seriously hurt."

"At least I got it on file. Maybe that can buy me some time with the landlord if he sees I made an actual police report and knows I'm not lying about my rent being stolen."

We sat there for five minutes.

"Knock, knock."

Someone was at my front door. It was not a hard police knock, just a normal knock. Ana and I looked at one another, sketched out. "Who's that?" we both wondered curiously.

I jumped back off the couch and opened the door. It was the same police. What were they doing?

"Hello?"

"Hi, you called?"

"Um... ya. You were just here. You left."

"No," the guys said, looking at one another, "we just got here."

"What?" I said, shaking my head.

"You reported that you had an intruder?"

"Yea... but you guys were just here, and you left," I said, standing by the door holding it open.

"No we weren't," the cops said, agreeing with one another.

"Yes you were." I was not going to argue, and I let them back in.

Ana and I stared at one another, uncomfortable. What was going on?

"You said you couldn't help me, that there was nothing you could do."

"What would you like us to do?"

I stood there for a moment thinking, "Well, I would like you to ask my neighbours if they saw or heard anyone."

"Why don't you come with us?"

This was getting stranger by the minute.

"Okay," I agreed and confidently led the way out of my place. We walked across the hallway. I knocked. No answer.

"Um, okay, well let's go upstairs and ask."

"You knock on the door."

"You want me to knock?"

"Yes. Wait. What are you going to ask them?"

"Well, I'm going to ask if they heard or saw anything downstairs," I replied. I couldn't believe it—they were putting me in charge. Wow.

The two cops looked at each other then said, "Okay, ya, sounds good."

I walked around them and up the next four steps.

"Knock, knock."

When the door opened, I was surprised to see a mother. Now I had a face to match the voice. She had dark hair and was much taller than me. The door really held back the noise of screaming children.

"Hello, my name is Joy. I live downstairs."

"Hi. I'm Darcy, what can I do for you?" I looked back to the police and they nodded for me to go ahead. "I was wondering if you've seen or heard anything downstairs that was unusual today?"

"Yes. I thought I heard you."

"You did?" I was surprised.

"What happened? Do you know?"

"I thought I heard you screaming."

I looked back at the two cops, jolted.

"It sounded like you were yelling, "Get out of my place." I heard you. You were swearing at him loudly. Then I heard your neighbour's door slam shut."

"It was my neighbour?"

"Yes, I think so. I heard his door slam right after you yelled at him."

"Okay. Thank you so much."

"Now what?" I asked the police.

"Let's go back down and check again."

"Knock, knock."

We stood there waiting. The door slowly opened. My claws dug in for the blood when my neighbour opened his door.

"Did you come into my place today?"

"No." He shook his head.

"Well someone did. They took all my rent money."

"It wasn't me. Sorry."

I glared at him, and he shut his door. I turned to the police, who now felt more like caring friends. "Thanks for helping me."

"Keep your door locked. Okay? It's not safe."

"Okay, I will. Thanks."

How could I have blacked out and defended myself at the same time? Every time I crashed, it was always for days. No one could ever wake me up. People would bang on my door for hours and I slept right through all the noise.

I walked back into my place and closed the door. Nothing made sense. What ever did happen, I'm waiting to find out one day. God was watching over me. I was very thankful that nothing worse had happened. Thank you, Lord, for protecting me.

I went to the bank and pulled out cash. I was aware I was spending all my proceeds of crime.

At a later date, I ran into Drades across town. He smiled at me, and I got as far away from him as I could. I went home and changed my door locks again. I barricaded my place so no one could get in or out. I was frantic with fear. He had the eyes of a clown. Such "sadness" was a twisted display of manipulation. I hoped for him, but he was another one of those types that I had to protect myself from. No matter how much you want to believe, it's better off you don't. Nonetheless, it was sad to later hear he had hung himself in jail.

Shortly there after, at about 10:30 p.m., I was cleaning my place and rubbing all the black fingerprints off the furniture. In between cleaning, I was doing my laundry. The washer was right outside my door, so I never locked it.

Two strangers walked right into my place. I was startled. For a change, I was friendly. I pointed across the hall, telling them, "No, you got the wrong place."

The girl was stalky and speedy, and headed right for me. I didn't realize what was going down. She punched me in the face and started walloping me with her fist. Crack! Crack! Blood started to gush out of my nose. She pushed me down on the couch and jumped on top of me. I squirmed underneath her, trying to break free; but she had my arms pinned down. I needed to get my leg out. My raw energy burst into overdrive, and it was on. Hostile rage surged in my blood, stimulating the electric currents to my brain. I was overcharged. My adrenaline ignited a kill switch and I freed my leg to get it underneath her. With one leg, I lifted her entire body up off of me, and sent her flying across the room. She crashed down against my coffee table, tumbling over with a loud thud. Now they were the ones surprised. I rose up like a phoenix to take command of this entire situation. The guy had jacked me. He took one look at me bleeding. She got up, and they both ran away like cowards.

I slammed my front door, shut and locked it!

I was bleeding profusely.

Blood, blood, and more blood.

I was surprised I was still human, and that blood actually flowed in my veins. I sat down, hating life.

My nose was broken. I had two black eyes, and I had had enough. These people could all jump off a cliff and get their own dope. I was done selling drugs, permanently. Never again. If I kept selling drugs, I would get killed. These people were crazy.

I started a sensible nine to five job. On my day off, I planned to bike down to the glass store and buy some Pyrex so I could blow a glass pipe. I had been up all night and headed over to the Science and Laboratory store, sketched out. I hated being sketchy.

I grabbed my bike. The brakes were not working on it, but I didn't feel like working on them just then. I needed glass, and I needed to go or the day would pass me by.

The day was like any other day in the city. The architecture of the buildings had curb appeal that held its own among the loudness of the hustle of traffic that yielded to little miss pretty please. There was nothing like the city, and me in it. I belonged there, and there was nothing more meaningful in that moment, except being a part of it – something bigger, larger than life. My thoughts of grandeur filled my head as I rode through the streets. I gained confidence like a super-woman, like truly nothing could stop me. I was capable of anything, whether my brakes worked or not. The voice encouraged my greatness.

I was less than two minutes from the glass store. I just had to go down this steep hill and then around this fence and I was there. Unless I biked straight off this drop off, then I didn't need to go around the fence. I could do it. No problem. There was nothing I could not do on that bike; my power was infinite. I had done little tricks on my bike that I thought made me look cute and all, but a fifteen-foot drop off onto a solid concrete parking lot was much more than I had ever bargained for. I went and took it, full speed ahead, like a champ, until I got right up to it. Then I was reminded,

I have no brakes.

That was enough. I hesitated and went crashing down hard.

I don't remember the lights going out, but I do remember lights going on, but only for a second. People working at the store came running out to help me. 911 was called, and I managed to say, "I can't afford an ambulance." I could not move and went back into unconsciousness.

I woke up later that evening in searing pain from head to toe. Where was I? I felt trapped in my body and couldn't move. My head was pounding with a throbbing pain. The place smelled so clean. What was all the beeping noise about? I heard low whispers in the background. I tried to move but lay stuck. What had happened to me that I was so stiff? I started swearing, and I found out I was not alone in the room.

"Stop swearing! This is a hospital. You need to be respectful."

"Well, what's wrong with me? What happened?"

"You fractured your skull and broke your collar bone."

"Ouch! It hurts so much..."

"We had to give you ten stitches above your left eye."

I tried to move but was helpless. I felt like I was nailed down to the bed.

"Listen here, if you swear again, you can leave. This is your final warning!" The nurse ordered. Why was she so mean? I really had no other words for the pain I felt. Here I lay in searing pain. I could have died, and she was giving me a lecture about swearing? I tried to move an inch and swore out loud again. Had they not given me painkillers? The nurse had zero tolerance for me and my language. I must have looked messed up, and with that, the nurse kicked me out of the hospital. I was so upset at her for all her attitude. I had no choice but to get up and leave, no matter how much it hurt. I guess they didn't have patience for junkies. I was still a person. I still had feelings.

I left the hospital pretending that I didn't need them or their help. I would have wanted my mom to be there. I missed Mom and my family more than ever. I limped along, a total mess, coming to realize that I had nothing in this city. All I could do was hobble one step at a time with a bike that had somehow made it with me to the hospital. It had been parked at the emergency exit back door. I put my weight on it and used it as a walker to slide me along.

I was angry, hurting, and this was going to be a long walk home with no help. Oh, how I wished I were still lying in the hospital. I needed to be taken care of, but now all I needed was to get high. If I was high, I would be able to walk. I could easily endure this intense pain.

I watched the traffic pass by me on the city streets and cursed at all of them. The buildings didn't seem so grand anymore – they were just buildings, and I was nothing more than a junkie.

I leaned over my bike and put my right arm across my handle bar to support my left leg because I couldn't use it at all. I was not thankful to be alive or that people helped me by calling the ambulance.

I had crashed in front of Vital Air, a business that sold oxygen. They had witnessed the entire accident and hooked me up with air just before I went into unconsciousness. At the hospital, they stitched me up, reset my collarbone, and put it in a sling. No, being thankful had not crossed my mind. I was consumed with my pain and the aggravation of walking all this way.

The further along I got, the more helpless I felt. This was the worst possible situation I could get myself into, and the negativity inside me was burning until I was full of rage. I would have loved to scream at anyone, but I had to settle for the pavement.

It took hours, and I noticed the moon passing over me before I finally got home, which led to another problem – stairs. I wheeled my GT LTX to the edge. She was a metallic silver, A-frame, and custom-built for me. I had started buying dope from a guy across town, and he had bike frames one dreamed of. I let her go, and she went clanking down each stair loudly and then crashed down with a thud. Oh, that was painful to watch. I gripped the step railing and used my core to move myself awkwardly down the steps.

The neighbour lady, Darcy, heard me coming back home and freaked out with concern when she saw me. She helped me by letting me use her cordless phone.

My apartment was trashed with clothes everywhere, and my furniture was disorganized. There was broken glass on the floor and clutter piled everywhere. I made my way over to the bed and I crashed out for a few hours. This guy Chelmer came to my window and woke me up. I had his cell phone, and I had to give it back to him. He knocked, and when he saw me, he cursed.

"What happened?"

I could barely sit up, so I reached over, and handed him his phone. I couldn't get up to answer my door to let him in, and I handed him his phone through the window, then crashed.

I woke up the next morning in pain. I slowly managed to lift my head, so I could see what was on my bed – clothes and tools. I was lying on a heap of things. I put my head back down and rested. I needed to go to the washroom. I tried to get up, but a weight of a truck felt like it was on top of me. It hurt, and I couldn't move. I was upset. I hated being helpless. I hated it with everything in me. I needed to get high and managed to move my one arm to my bag and get it over to me. I grabbed my pipe and put it in my mouth. I grabbed a lighter and tried to light it.

I was useless, I couldn't do it. I didn't have the strength. Zero. How was this possible? If I could just get high, I could break through this threshold of pain. Man, there must be someone I could call to come over.

I grabbed the phone and tried Tdo, but he wasn't there. I tried Scott and Ana, but they were not home either, and no one else knew where I lived. Great. The pressure was building. I needed to go to the washroom. Purely out of desperation, I dialed the only number I had left.

"Hello?"

"Hey, Mom." Her voice was familiar and sweet in my ears.

"Hi Joy, how are you? I haven't heard from you in a long time."

"Oh Mom. I'm in a lot of pain. I just got out of the hospital. I was in a bike accident."

"Are you okay? Where are you?" she was frantic with worry, I could hear it in her voice.

"Um, I'm at home now, but I can't move. I broke my collarbone and my leg feels completely mangled. I'm okay, it's just that...I really have to go to the washroom, but I can't for the life of me move, except my right hand slowly. Other than that, my strength has completely left me. I really hate to bother you, but I need help."

"We will be right there, okay. Do you need me to bring anything?"

"Really?" I was surprised that she did not even hesitate.

"Um, like no. I just need a hand up. Thanks Mom. I will be lying on my bed. The door is unlocked." I closed my eyes and waited for my parents.

When they walked through my door, I was embarrassed from my prodigal living conditions.

"Joy, you're coming home with us," Dad said firmly.

I didn't argue. My parents had to call the ambulance back to my place to help lift me up. I was in excruciating pain. I was a mess.

NINE

EXECUTIVE DECISIONS

My brain was starting to feel like mush. The static in my head was a normal state, and things were really disconnecting. I was on system overload, and the motherboard in my brain was short-circuiting. The wires must have been over-stimulated and burnt up from the excruciatingly painful walk a few nights earlier. My body slept for days, doing major repair work.

My plan was to head back to Calgary as soon as I could walk. I told my boss Natalie I would be back as soon as possible. I wasn't planning on letting her down, but at the same time, I really needed to take a break from the hostile cynicism. Of course, we users see ourselves as our own type of aristocrats. A family derived of the outcast and rejected. Our anthem invites the bigoted and unloved. We don't reject anyone, and there are no rules. If you didn't make it out there, you could make it in our world. Anyone can be king or queen, but eventually, everyone gets dethroned. It was a sharp juxtaposition from family suppers that were ready and waiting on the table and the feeling of being in good company.

A week or more had passed, and I was ready to take the plunge.

"Um, like I need to get back to work. I feel much better now," I told Dad.

"You're not going back, Joy." He looked at me with his soft caring eyes. The words gutted me. My biggest fears were about to come true; they had me trapped.

"Well like, I have a job and I have to go back. I live there. That's my home."

"If you go back there, you will die," Dad said as he shook his head and looked at me. "You are not going."

Tough love. Praise God. No doubt, I knew his words were true. Deep inside I knew it was all gone. This was the reason I had stayed far away from my family and from the executive decisions that always cast a ballot without my vote.

"We need to find you a place to get help," Mom said.

I took a final look, viewing everything I held in my hands, and let it go. My past, the people, using drugs, and so much evil were all going to become distant memories. I looked ahead at my wonderful parents. How could I have any regrets or not be thankful to be back among the living with a heart and soul that beat again? I was slowly feeling emotions of genuine love. I was coming back to life thanks to my parents.

In no time, two weeks had passed, and I had a new lease on life – and God started to sew the seams. The heat breaking from the dawn is the impetus that bursts the new skin. Regeneration from the peak gives way to the mountain ice, it slowly melts down the summit into the valley. Follow the trickling of the spring dripping down into a hidden chasm and take another step. There you'll see the water's propagation. Trace the small creatures moving from the current into the deep. It all eventually flows out into the Great Lakes. This is life coming back into reconciliation.

I needed redemption, and I was on the right path. For so long I had been caught up. Invested, but never disciplined. I tended to forget that life has a way of making miracles according to the genetic codes of wisdom and DNA. Only a mind of superiority and intellect could specifically design such a vast arrangement of blueprints creating life. Well, if I had a blueprint created from some DNA code that God had woven, then maybe there was a plan already woven for my future. I could not help but think that the past was history and the future only God knew. That is His right and glory. If for God the future has already been, then I must be here for His glory. I'm not the one with the infinite understanding of a trillion zeros after you put a one in front of them all. Numbers too big just don't make sense to me. Do they make sense to anyone really? Who can grasp it? Who has that kind of comprehension but the one who created such endless possibilities? To think, we could potentially make that many choices throughout one lifetime, and God tracks them all...wow. What an amazing God.

I looked into the new life that had been created while I had been away, and I saw the work of God's design. My sister's children were all so special.

Shaun was always over at my parents' house while Nathan was at school. Shaun had blond hair, and he was always smiling.

"Hey auntie, I brought you breakfast in bed."

"Oh Shaun...you're such a sweetheart," I said sitting up in bed.

His bright green eyes were filled with love. He was clumsy, which made him all the cuter, having constant bumps and ban-aids. He smiled down at me. He was missing his front tooth. "Can I eat your eggs?" He loved eggs.

"Yes, you can. I will have the toast. This is so sweet of you! Thank you."

"Can you teach me how to ride my bike today? I brought it over," he said excited.

I was just as excited to teach him; it was a privilege.

"I would love to! Let's do that." I had missed life and was soaking it up.

By the end of the month, my parents took me to a homeless shelter in Edmonton called the James Spady. It offered much love and compassion to broken people who had burned all their bridges and were feeling pretty low. We had blown it in life so many times, which reduced us to feeling much less in life then what we actually were. I felt at home there. It was us against the world mind set.

I was on my third week there when I got a phone call from my Remi. She was still fighting for me. It made me feel like my old normal self to be able to carry on a conversation with her. We were on the same side. My walls were down and I felt enthusiastic. Remi held none of my faults against me. I was thankful that she was always looking out for me.

"Hello?" I answered, standing in the hallway.

My arm was in a sling. I was wearing baggy jeans with pockets and a dark grey and pink T-shirt. My hair was now long and dark. But my newest feature I had going for me now was stitching – a scar above my left eye.

"Hi, how are you?" Remi asked.

"I'm doing pretty good. Me and the boys down here are watching playoffs. I'm still waiting to go to treatment."

"How would you feel if I told you we found a place for you to go?"

"You did? I'm waiting to go to a place here. Like where were you thinking?"

"Well, it's in Quebec."

"Woe...are you serious?" Not even in my dreams did I have thoughts of this place.

"It is a private rehab in Les Trois-Rivières. It's called Narcanon. Have you ever heard of it?"

"Nope. I haven't heard of it. I never would go to any institution that's called "Narc". So, what has you sniffing up this tree?" I didn't think my parents had money to burn like this. Besides, I was well. Remi took a moment reading over the information she had gathered about Narcanon and gave me the most relevant information I needed to know about the place so I could make an informed decision.

"They guarantee they can fix you, and that you will never relapse ever again."

"How can they do that?"

"They deal with the underlying issues, not just the addiction."

"Um, ya, I don't speak French and like I don't have any underlying issues. I'm just addicted."

"They speak English there too."

"Like are you serious? You want to send me halfway across the world?"

"It's not about that; they guarantee your recovery."

I thought about everything Remi was saying... "Um, well how long do I stay there for?"

"As long as you like. Start with six months."

"This sounds like it costs lots."

"Ya, it does. It's $20,000."

"Are you serious! Who is going to pay for this?"

"Joy, don't worry about it. Mom and Dad will do anything for you."

"Well, when would I leave?" I wasn't in a huge hurry to take off.

"Tomorrow."

"Tomorrow! Like this is happening kinda fast. I have to pack."

"So, will you go?"

It was a once-in-a-lifetime opportunity; how could I not jump at it? "Um, sure, yes. Thanks!"

I hung up the receiver, excited, and turned to the TV room, throwing up my one good hand and announcing, "I'm getting out of here, boys!"

"Where are you going Joy?" I felt the wave of disappointment.

"Quebec!" and I turned around and hobbled to my room.

Mom and I spent the next day packing. I was going to miss my family. I loved my parents, and I could see I had done them so wrong. I was looking forward to being their daughter again. I felt truly happy inside. As for tomorrow, I did not want to be woken up in the middle of the night, so I grabbed a blanket to take to sleep in the truck. All things were still when I jumped in the back seat and shut the door. I looked up. I did not move a muscle. I was horrified and did not make a sound.

TEN
WHERE DID YOU
SEND ME?

It was him again... the Joker. Was I seeing things? I closed my eyes, remaining calm and rational, and then I opened them again. He was standing right in front of me, watching me. Were my eyes playing tricks on me? I turned and looked over to the left at the pine tree. It was the same old pine tree that had been there for years. I thought when I looked back, the Joker would be gone. But the Joker was still right there.

I sit still, gripping on tightly to the seat in front of me; what was going on? He leaned against the door of my dad's garage. I could see his face. His eyes were like two black slits of evil that pressed through me. Shooting glares of deaths scorn at me. He was of a darker complexion, and this time, he had white face paint on instead of a hard-white mask. His face structure was thin and long, with highly defined cheekbones. He had the perfect huge smile that went from ear to ear, with straight white teeth. The corners of his mouth curled up. He was picture perfect. He wore the court jester hat; it had a bell on the end of it. Something about his outfit told me he despised having to wear it. His arms were crossed against his chest. To my horror, he started laughing at me, uncontrollably.

I froze with fear. Was this the beast right in front of me? What was he doing here? The night had come calling, but I swear, this time, I hadn't provoked it. No. I had to get out of this truck! He was trying to intimidate me. Why, why, why? Well, he could stand there and laugh all he wanted from night to dawn and from day to night. Twisted and sadistic thrills were his pleasures, but not mine. I was out of there! I jumped out of the truck and ran as fast as I could to the patio door, which was the closest way inside the house and never looked back. I was safe inside and shut the door behind me. I ran into my parents' bedroom, nudging Mom lightly.

"Mom... shhhh come here," I whispered, grabbing her arm.

She rose up startled and I held on. We went in the living room and in my panic and utter fear, I let the tears loose.

"I just saw the Joker outside in front of the truck when I went out there. He was standing right in front of me, Mom. He was laughing at me. He was trying to frighten me." I told her, chilled to the bone.

Mom was confused. What was going on?

Mom woke up Dad, and they looked outside the kitchen window, then through the patio door, but no one was there.

"It was the devil. He was dressed as the court jester. He was right in front of your garage," I said, shaking my head back and forth mesmerized. Mom and Dad looked at each other and didn't say a word, but the expression was written on both their faces. I couldn't expect them to believe me. I continued on with some sort of explanation to what he was doing there as best as I could understand.

"I think he was trying to scare me into not going to that rehab place, but he should know me better than that. I'm not going to let him win. I'm going for sure now," I said, trying to be brave and defiant against the night.

Mom and I slept together on the couch that night. I was way too upset to be alone and didn't want her to leave my side. For the first time in a long while, I felt vulnerable. I didn't know the future, and once again, I was leaving my family.

Up in an airplane, how high do these things go? I wondered if I had ever been so high on drugs? Ha, ha, ha. Probably higher! Ha, ha, ha. I laughed to myself, feeling pretty proud. I looked out the window. I could see my reflection in the window and admired. Wow, my hair really looked gorgeous. The feeling was summer hot. Humidity was at its peak, and things were just sticking to me. My shirt, the air around me, and the heat made my hair look like it had about ten extra inches of body.

I walked off the boarding ramp and over to the luggage station to pick up my bags. I found two guys sticking out like a sore thumb. Happy, giddy, both short. They made their acquaintance with me, scooped up my luggage. We picked up another addict up at the airport. And we were off.

I sat in the back seat and took in the loudness around me. It did not take me long to figure out everyone who drives in Quebec is crazy. The traffic was suicidal; people were running stop signs like they did not exist. Everyone cut each other off, honking their horns. There really seemed to be no traffic laws, and there was one speed – fast. The two men talked in French. I had no clue what they were saying. I just buckled up and held on.

"Hi, my name is Joy."

He smiled at me, "Hi, I'm Kevin."

He was tall, thin, and had brown eyes. He seemed kinda delicate, but boyish.

"What are you in for?"

"Cocaine. And you?"

"Crystal."

"How is you're with drawl? How many days sober are you?"

"I slept the entire flight. I went out blazin all week. You?"

"I'm sober about a month. I actually feel great."

"That is great. These people are crazy hey." We laughed together in the back seat.

"Ya." And we smiled on.

I had never been to rehab, but I got an instant strange feeling about the place; it felt shady. I thought to myself, "this is it?" We pulled up, and there were many buildings. The first was an old church that was now purposed for intake and detox. There was another building further off, which looked big and gloomy. That building was for people on the methadone program, which was for people coming off of heroin. Another big building was the main stage. All administration was upstairs, and the main floor was dining, where people hung out. Downstairs were the classrooms. Another separate building housed the sauna program and separate living quarters for men and ladies.

I arrived there, and it was anything but conventional. I followed the men and was shuffled around and admitted. The people there looked to be mostly my age, twenty-six or younger. Next, they did a full strip-search of myself. It was uncomfortable; then next to my temporary living quarters, detox. I was already detoxed, so it was strange why I could not just get started with the program. I had nothing to sleep off, and I was raring to go, but they held me back. They told me they had exercises with my mind to do and so on.

The detox building was small – a long hallway with lots of lonely rooms. Halfway down the hall, I saw a girl lying on her stomach. I casually watched as I walked by. She was lying face down, on a special looking table. Guys were touching her all over her body, chanting slowly: "Feel my hands, feel my hands, feel my hands, feel my hands..." over and over again. Creepy. I walked by, pretending like I thought it was totally normal. *Why were they doing that?* I thought to myself. How uncomfortable for that girl. What did having to be touched all over the body have to do with getting off drugs? Well, they didn't understand. They could not just expect me to lie down and surrender my body over to them for this strange type of treatment. No, this place was not practical for helping addicts, at least that was the impression I got. Freaky. What kind of nut joint was I in? A loony bin? A psych ward?

I was apprehensive but kept walking cautiously down the long hallway. *This place is feeling stranger by the minute,* I thought to myself unnerved, running my hands through my hair. It felt spooky. In the next room, there were two chairs facing each other. An older gentleman was sitting across from a younger one. The older man was guiding the younger one in a slow, repetitive trance. They chanted over and over, "*Open your mind...open your mind...open your mind.*" The words alarmed me instantly. That one little phrase gave me tingling shivers down the back of neck. Red flags were waving in front of my face and loud sirens started sounding.

All the uneasy feelings that went straight to my heart were officially confirmed. I was in danger.

All those years ago, when I was a little girl, sitting in church, Pastor Bob warned the congregation, "You must never open your mind to the world, you have to protect it." And I knew; this place was a cult.

The Holy Spirit grabbed my attention immediately, putting me on high alert. I was all alone and far from family. There was no one to call, and I was about to be locked up. Everything made sense to me, including seeing the Joker. He was the warning the night before I had left to come to this place...this place was evil! This place was weird! A bunch of crazy loonies! Was this just another layer in the Joker's den?

ELEVEN

BRAINWASHED

Detox facilitators would not let me leave or make a phone call. The first exercise I had to do was sitting down on a chair. Surprise, surprise. I would have to repeat to them everything I saw in the room for hours. That was the beginning of my brainwashing. I refused to open my mind, and they held me back in detox longer than anyone. New people would come and go, and I was sober but stuck in detox playing mind games.

The worst for me, and everyone else least favourite exercise, was when we would have to sit face-to-face in front of one another, staring into one each others eyes. You were not allowed to look away for five whole minutes. You were not allowed to blink, smile, or change your facial expression. When I looked into my partner's eyes, at first, he looked fine. But the longer I held the stare, the more uncomfortable it became. I seen such hurt within him, it was not right. I was able to look under all the layers. The longer I stared, the further I looked inside his soul. His eyes began to water, like he was asking for mercy. He was weak, vulnerable, and a scared child, and we both started to tremble. We both wanted to blink or look away, but we were forbid not to, and tears welled up in both our eyes.

"Why do we have to do this?" I complained to my partner Kevin after we were done. It couldn't get more awkward than that. A shattered soul in a broken human. The intensity of the situation made it very personal, like we were connected in a very deep, spiritual way. After the exercise, my partner said I had kind eyes, and I thanked him, not sure what to tell him about his. I had glued myself to his stare. I searched down deep in his brown eyes. It required bravery to face his fears. His eyes started to vibrate and I kept staring, intently intrigued. Should I tell him, "I just watched you break. You were helpless and damaged, from the centre of your soul." I never wanted to make eye contact with another human as long as I lived. I was starting to twitch with awkwardness and discomfort. I had seen too many broken souls over my lifetime. Vulnerability and fear was becoming one and the same. It was an incredibly hard thing to feel, and so was being weak. I was afraid to see any more pain.

At the end of the week, Kevin was released into the main program. He was detoxed. I apparently was not.

I needed to know more about this place; it seemed weird to me. I started investigating and asking more questions about the facility and their methods of practice. They were the ones being sketchy, and I wanted to know what was going on. They sent in one of the top directors to come talk to me. She was dressed to kill, wearing an expensive outfit, and she had her hair and nails done. She was easy to talk to and I opened right up to her. I decided I better chill out or they would never let me out of the detox unit where I could get to a phone. The director promised me, "You will be out of the detox unit tomorrow, and I will be personally taking you under my wing."

The next day, my bags were packed. I was transferred into the normal dormitory with the other girls. I needed to get to a phone to call home and tell my parents that this place gave me the heebie jeebies. *Okay, think,* I told myself. How do I tell them what I need to say and have them actually believe me? Tread thoughtfully.

CLEAVE TO JESUS CHRIST

I called Mom and delicately unfolded a picture of the place, the weird things that had happened, and the funny feelings I had.

"Mom, I will totally stay here and do the program, but I don't think you would agree with what is going on here. I think this place is a cult."

Mom never said much. We got off the phone and I told her I would call her later.

The next day I woke up. The weather was hot. I walked over to the building and met up with my friend Kevin for breakfast.

"How was your night? What do you think of the place?" I asked.

He leaned in at the table and grinned. "Ya, this place is sketchy hey? I did not have a good sleep at all."

"Have you talked to your mom?" I asked.

He ran his hand through his hair, still grinning, and looked around, "Ya, but just for like, a minute. I am going to call her later today."

"Did you tell her what you thought about the place?"

"I told her I thought it was weird."

"Dude, I think we need to get out, before they brainwash us. I'm sure it is a cult."

"Ya. I definitely think so too."

"Where else would you go for treatment?"

"I'm not sure. Maybe Edmonton."

"Ya, I was supposed to go to Edmonton myself, and than my sister found this place."

We both got up and put our dishes away. I headed back to my room and prepared for the day.

I got a tall stack of brightly coloured new school textbooks. I would be starting in a classroom with the others. This place seemed more messed up then the drugs I had done. The books were big. On the front cover it said, "L. Ron Hubbard." Okay. That must be the guy who founded the program. I opened up the textbook. Weird. Every page had a basic picture, a large font, and three to four words per sentence. I start flipping through the pages. This was odd. It said nothing about drugs. I wondered about what all the other people there thought about the program. If I had to discern, it seemed like these were books like you would get as a child when you were beginning to learn how to read. To me, it seemed like they were trying to reprogram our brains. Great. I slammed the textbook shut. I didn't want any part in it.

"Hey Kevin, check these books out. What do you think?"

Kevin flipped through the pages. "Weird. These books and this place are strange."

Once we were finished the ten or twelve children's books, we would advance into the sauna sessions. There we spent over six hours a day, for a few months, sweating in a hot sauna. You were given water, drug bombs. I do not know what was in the drug bombs they were giving us. But it was lots of them at a time. We were given Niacin to help "flush" all the drugs out of our system. Only a few people had died from the sauna. All the addicts were saying how awesome the experience was: "It was enlightening! The sauna is the best!" Everyone was ecstatic. Hmm. Hours later, Kevin motioned to me.

"Well, maybe this place isn't that terrible."

"Are you serious? Just a few hours ago you thought it was. Are you changing your mind?"

I was worried. He was getting sucked in.

Maybe I was being overly paranoid. No one else there seemed to be having any problem with the place.

At night, I lay down in bed. I thought I could hear sounds that I could not make out. The most mysterious noises I thought came across the way, in the other big five-storey building where the methadone program was. I had never seen anyone ever come out of that building. My mind was going over all these questions that I did not have answers for. Hopefully, I would eventually get some sleep, if I could just stop thinking. My mind raced with non-stop thoughts that would not subside.

The next day I called my parents back, and I was surprised. My mom answered the phone. "Joy, we are so sorry." I listened closely. *Why is she sorry,* I thought, with my ear glued to the phone.

"Is there anyone around you listening in?" I looked around. Just the usual. Why was she acting so sketchy?

"What is going on Mom?"

Mom did not hesitate to tell me. "You're in a cult."

"What?"

How could they have sent me here?

"We looked into it some more. There are a lot of horror stories about that place. Are you okay?"

Horror stories? Great. The sounds I hear at night... Maybe something far more nefarious was going on than I could ever imagine. No wonder I had seen the devil the night before I had left. He was not laughing because he was trying to intimidate or frighten me. He was laughing because I was being sent to this cult halfway across the country. He figured he had me beat.

"Dad and Ken are going to come and get you out of there, okay? Don't say anything to anyone, just hold on."

"Right. Are you serious? Is it that evil?" I asked, raising my eyebrows, leaning into the receiver.

"Yes, it is."

"I'm glad Dad doesn't have to come alone. The traffic is crazy. I will warn you right now."

I steadfast found Kevin. "Dude! My dad is coming to get me! This place is a cult. For sure. When they come tomorrow, you can leave with us."

"Like, are you serious? They are actually coming all that way?" he smiled.

"You like the place now? Don't you?"

"Is it that heinous?"

"Dude, I think it is. I won't leave you here."

"Okay, I will go with you."

I sauntered back to my room. My mind replayed back to the morning I was sitting in church as a little girl. I must have been eight years old. It seemed like God planned that service for this moment in my life. *"Never open your mind. You have to protect it."* Without that specific warning, I would have zero clue I was in major danger. It proved to me that God knew my future and was looking out for me. God knew about this place and that one day I would come here. God had prearranged the warning of a lifetime. Thank you, God. You have never failed me.

The next day, Dad and Ken were in Quebec at Narcanon, just like they said they would be.

Dad and Ken wanted their money and were up in the administration offices dealing with things.

I was in the hallway and overheard my dad coming unglued.

"This is not a treatment centre! This is the church of *Scientology,* and you are a *cult!* You guys lied to us, and we want our money back! Joy is leaving with us today!"

I had never heard my dad yell before, especially at strangers. The people did not want to let me leave. Ken and Dad stormed out of the office. We made a scene. I was glad for the fact that the other addicts would be warned that the place was evil. I hoped that they would have parents who they could call and get out. I grabbed Kevin and we followed close behind. We went straight to the rental car and hopped in the backseat.

"You are my heroes! Thank you for getting me out of that place. I didn't think I would be seeing you so soon." I was relieved.

They both looked at me. Ken was the cheeky type and was about to let loose on what he thought of the place. "They prey on people who are desperate for help. They don't tell people it is Scientology at all.

Remi looked all night and day for information about the place, and the more we looked, the more frightening stories started appearing."

"Well, I'm so grateful. I'm glad you believed me."

"We almost didn't," Dad said, which surprised me.

"What?"

"Well, the night you got there, they called us and talked to Mom. They told us, "Expect a phone call from your kid telling you that the place is weird and that it is a cult. They said, kids are going to do this because they are paranoid, and it is just the drugs playing with their mind or they want to leave. Do not believe them. It is totally normal.""

"What! Are you serious? So, you knew I was going to call and tell you that it was a cult before I actually ever did? Wow, how deceptive."

"Yes. We didn't believe you at first. But we remembered the night before you left how you said you saw the Joker outside. We just thought you were paranoid, but it suddenly all made sense."

Woe. It all felt surreal sitting in the back of the car. I was in shock that I was safe from the grip of impending madness. I was rescued from something that could have turned out so differently. "Thanks for not leaving me there. I appreciate what you guys did for me. I love you both."

Ken piped up, "This traffic is crazy! These people drive like idiots! I'm never coming back to Quebec ever again, and it is the last place in the world I would want to go."

"I second that!"

"I'm thankful too- that I don't have to drive. Ha, ha, ha, ha," Dad said laughing to himself; and then it was silent in the car. We were all paying attention to the cars whipping by us. There was no sanity here.

We got a hotel room. Dad and Ken crashed.

Kevin and I stayed up talking the entire night. Realizing we probably would never see each other again. We had got close in a short time.

"So, where are you going to go?" I looked at Kevin.

"I booked a flight back to Winnipeg."

"Do you know if you are going to go back to treatment?"

"I will. Maybe I will try to come to Edmonton. I will look you up when I get there. Okay?"

"Ya. That will be nice. I will miss you."

"I will miss you too. Here is my phone number. Call me?"

"Yes. I will give you mine too."

Before the dawn we parted ways. We had the first flight out. A little sad to leave him. I wanted nothing but the best for him and wished him well on his journey.

A week or so after I got home, I went to the church. I got my previous youth pastor Tim to meet with me to pray. I confessed my past and asked God for forgiveness. I had many people praying for me that night. We prayed for the protection of my life and thanked God. I left the church that evening feeling lighter. My eyes were different when you looked into them.

I thought it best I take a more sensible approach to treatment.

The door to the AADDAC building was heavy and always kept shut. The place was neat and orderly like what my life was starting to look like. I sat down at a small round table and filled out a questionnaire form. I was introduced to Ruby. She was short and petite with blonde hair, green eyes, and a calming voice. Her genuine concern made her easy to open up to. I relax and tell her my story.

Ruby replied, "I understand how you would want to shut off all your feelings. It must have been very hard. You are a very sensitive girl. There are healthy ways to deal with coping with your problems so that you do not need to turn to drugs, which actually make it worse."

"Ya, my oldest sister says I need to find my identity, but I don't know how."

"That is another thing you will learn as you get clean. These things will take time. You need to learn who you are and what is important to you. You really stop maturing when you use drugs. Although you are twenty-seven, you actually stopped maturing at the age when you started using. So, if you started using at age seventeen, your brain stops developing, and you stay at that maturity level. It will take time before your brain will be healed and catch up."

"Wow. That makes sense. I feel really awkward and very immature. I definitely am behind in life."

I like how she can somehow see some good in me. She does not judge me.

"I will give you a work book. You can take it home with you, then bring it back next time, and we will go over it together while you wait to go to treatment. There are lots of good ones to go to."

I didn't miss a beat. "I want to go to Calgary, to Aventa." I had been planning a way to get back to Calgary, and this might be my ticket.

She looks at me soberly, "It is your decision, but do you think that is a good idea?" she said, looking up at me with her pen in her hand and notebook in front of her.

She was probably right. This might be risky, but I felt assured about it.

I ended up at Aventa, a women's treatment centre in Calgary. It was about to be renovated. I stayed for almost eleven months in total. I was not certain how I would feel about being back there. I was in recovery with people who I used to sell drugs to. One girl, Joan, she was very paranoid and angry at me.

Joan and I were sitting down, she had one main question on her mind.

"Did you sleep with my boyfriend?"

I almost laughed. "No. I promise you, I never."

She sat there thinking. "He was always down in Forest Lawn. He always was talking about you. Are you sure?"

"I never slept with your boyfriend."

"I just think you did."

"I would never sleep with him."

"Where is he?"

"I have not seen Sam for a few months. He lives in Edmonton now."

I looked at Joan. She was eight months pregnant with Sam's baby.

"What about your baby?"

"I want him to be there."

"It must be tough. You are very strong. Will your baby be healthy?" Her pain will be deep.

"I pray. I depend on my faith to get me through this. I love Sam so much. I want to be with him. But, he cheated on me all the time."

"I promise you, I only sold drugs to him. I think you are better off without him."

Joan was up and down. Sometimes she seemed like she had it together, and the next, she was ready to fall apart.

In the classroom sessions we sat in small groups. We opened up and shared our experiences with one another; teaching us communication. We studied each behaviour, and the non-productive cycle of anger. A good facilitator asks the tough and touchy questions, made you feel uncomfortable, and pushed your boundaries. They had to pry to get in, and they set us off. This was not done in cruelty, but with extreme caution and professional integrity. It got heated in the rooms. Often times someone blew up in anger, that opened a door, and then we started talking. I remember the girls. Not so much their stories, but I remember their pain. The intimacy of opening up was like walking that high line wire. Our biggest fright; we were susceptible, with nothing to hold on to. Some girls were really hard inside, and they would not let anyone get close. Others were just lost and struggled to grasp who they were. It was hard to watch the ones who were battling themselves and realizing that I was no different.

We were all hunted by temptation, it seemed fun at first, until it begun ruining our lives. We had wandered our way and it had led us spiritually off course. We spent years being buried alive with fears. Our best invested resources: we used; we lived to be dead in our pain. With broken hearts we had become shut in prisoners, held back in isolation. Drugs are the devil's playground. And a sitting duck is prey for the enemy. We were caught in the hunter's traps who had come to seek, kill, and destroy our lives.

Treatment was a growing experience. So much to learn with great supports. It takes years to repair the damage done to a mind from drugs. God went before me. Everyday God guarded me from being triggered back into using. He is Faithful. The confidence I had when I had lived there before was lost to me. I rode around on my pedal bike, but it just felt aimless. I was not feeling indestructible.

I volunteered with the Calgary Distress Call Centre. Between nightly meetings, and training to help others, I was exhausted. Something pulled at me, maybe the wind was telling me it was time to go home. I had faced the city and never relapsed. I got the closure I needed. Nothing felt the same there any more. Maybe it was just me, and I left.

Finally, I made the last right-hand turn. I could see my parents' driveway and I pulled up in front of the house.

"Hi, Mom and Dad!"

"You're finally home! Come inside. Dad will grab your things."

Mom and I headed into the kitchen and were standing next to one another. I looked at Mom, who was such a beautiful woman, with gentle warm blue eyes. She looked back at me. I could tell she was savouring the sweet moment. The times she had me before were something that didn't last. She knew better. She knew the addiction always would take me back, and I'd be gone just as quick as I'd come back. Time was always something we treasured. She had hope, but she had disappointment. She had hurt. She had trust, but I always let her down. The stolen moments were devastation to a mother's heart. I knew what she was going to say because she had said it before. But this time she had waited, which made it all the sweeter.

She said smiling, "I have my daughter back." And how sweet it was. It had been so long, too long, so tough. But this time I did not relapse. This time I fought. This time, I was sure.

TWELVE
ALWAYS IN HIS HANDS

I applied for a job as a cashier. My boss was a tiny lady named Noreen. She had silver hair and a heart of gold. A woman of genuine kindness. It was like having a grandma. I walked in and handed her my resume, and she hired me on the spot. I got to know everyone who worked there, and it felt definitely more like a family than just a job. Noreen had been in town since the oil boom began, and she knew everyone in town. At first, she had sold insurance with her husband, Rusty. They had their own company, but then sold it to take over the Petroleum store. Their grandson Mason helped run the business.

Between work and home, I found time to get a playful puppy. A chocolate Lab cross. She was so cute. Every day I trained her and I loved her. I named her Piper. She was my coping tool. At seven months old, Piper was a naughty girl who escaped out of her pen. I looked everywhere for her. Dallas drove down the highway and a few minutes later, she was back with a look on her face that said it all.

"I'm so sorry, Joy."

I was devastated and walked over. Dallas slid open the heavy side door, and there was Piper. She had been hit by a car and was dead stiff. Dallas lifted Piper out of the van and set her gently into my arms. I carried her over to the grass under a tall, tree. I held her in my arms for a few hours crying. Death was taking over, but I didn't care.

Dad came and took stiff Piper from my arms. We buried her in the back field under a huge pine tree that was tall and had a lot of girth.

Reality was starting to get to me. Sure, there were warning signs. I chopped off all my long hair at work in the washroom. I did go to my supports, but they thought I was fine. Everyone in my family was dealing with grief. It was a season of deep pain and loss. A family member had died. Our world would be forever changed. For so long I had stayed strong, doing all I could to hold it together for my family and myself. The drugs were always somewhere. Addicts could be found easy enough, waiting for the right exact opportunity to show up. When you are vulnerable the devil always comes back, knocking on the door to see if you will answer.

My thoughts gravitated toward the easy fix. Why shouldn't I? No. Don't go there. I fought the urges with all the "willpower" I had. It is easy to relapse if you let your mind go there, and once you let your mind go there, you're at a high risk of relapsing. For those who live according to the flesh set their minds on the things of the flesh, but those who live according to the Spirit [set their mind on] the things of the Spirit. For to be carnally minded is death, but to be spiritually minded is life and peace. Romans 8:5-6

I ran into Chase. A boy I used with when I was much younger. I denied any wrongdoing. I was not hurting anyone, I justified. How could I be? I just happened to be at the wrong place at the wrong time, which pretty much set myself up for failure. Eventually, the opportunity would naturally present itself.

When I relapsed after over a year and half of being clean, liquid bombs from hell's grasp exploded within me. I felt instant deep regret. And once again, I was reminded that choosing to use drugs is the biggest mistake I could have made.

After an intense rush, I felt like I was the worst person alive. The evil took over my body, feeding off my soul. It returned as if it had missed me and knew I would be back if it waited long enough. The drug was my monomania, a pathological obsession with single idea, the old familiar that made me overwrought. I looked down at my arm to check my pulse. I thought my veins might as well turn from blue to black. I had lost my purple blood. My heart rate skyrocketed, running my body on a complete different level.

I needed immediate help and support. I was ashamed I had relapsed and kept the fact I had used a secret. No one could find out. I lay in bed downstairs in my bedroom, looking up at the ceiling. I was listening for any sounds. I was paranoid. I would sleep this one time off and hope to God I would not be back using again. Never again, I told myself. It was just one time.

I start dating Chase, a guy from my past. He loved baseball, fishing, and drugs. His life drowned in its own sorrows along the way. We climbed aboard into the same swamped boat. He had short brown hair, soft brown eyes, and unusual gentlemanly charm. We held different point of views on things like God, romance, and money, but we weren't confused about each other.

I should have just run some hot bathwater in a porcelain bathtub, dimmed the lights, lit a candle, put oodles of bubble bath in, and watched it all come undone.

"Knock, knock."

Once again, I was the one doing the knocking, asking for trouble.

I stood outside Lacy's trailer after work. Chase told me to come over. Lacy was Chase's older sister, they lived together.

I had liked him when I was eighteen years old. We had started seeing each other many years prior, but it fell apart through a big misunderstanding. My heart was open to him. I had no walls up. To me, he was that same guy I had known and liked.

"Come in."

Chase was lying on the blue sofa in the living room, relaxed.

"Hey, how are you?"

"I'm okay. How was work?"

"It was good. It's so nice out."

"Ya, I'm so tired."

"Um well, do you want to do something?"

I sit down on the chair in the living room.

"Like what?"

"I don't know."

"Hey babe, can we get some drugs?"

I was silent. I hated drugs. Drugs suck. So lame. *Oh great,* I think, rolling my eyes back in my head. I had only used once at this point. I didn't want to start using daily. I should have stayed away from him. But I liked him.

"No...we don't need drugs. I don't want to use."

I did not want to start slipping.

Could of, should of, would of. I could have walked away. I should have left. I would have known better. Years down the road, where did these choice lead?

"Well. I'm so tired."

"Are you serious?" I said, disappointed. "No. Come on. You don't need dope."

"Come on. Just this once. I'm so tired. If you get some drugs, I will feel better, then we can do whatever you want."

Well, would it be that big of a deal to get high?

"Just this once. I promise. I will feel so much better."

Maybe one more time wouldn't be that bad. I hated using last time. I didn't see myself getting hooked. I should be safe. I had this.

"Okay," I compromised. "But promise to not ask me again, okay? I don't want to get hooked again and start using all the time."

"Sure babe. Of course not," he said smiling.

Within three months, sad to say, I was right back down into the hole my family had dug me out of. It pushed me hard and sat me down fast. It was quicker than the crack of a whip. I was back in the scene. I tried my best to hold onto sobriety, but relapse is the same old song that lies and sings, "It is inevitable." Now, I was back with my feet in hell being buried alive. I guess I had never been fixed from the years of hurt. Life changes us all, deep within. The pain from a broken soul I do not know how long it takes to heal. It is tough.

I left my parents and moved in with Dallas for a bit. I was always with Chase and over at Lacy's place. Lacy had fair skin, light blue eyes; she was chill, and did not use drugs.

Chase and I had a bag of drugs and we went down to the river to go fishing. We took the trail through a winding path, where tall poplar trees and pines coexisted. Over the years, we had walked the path daily, keeping it trodden down to the clearing.

The sky dazzled its reflection against the truly spectacular river. This same river runs all the way right behind my grandparents' house in Saskatchewan. I had known it as a child. I remembered once loving those ways. Where purity was not conducive of the times. The only "rush" was the water, that ran along with wisdom, floating down inter-mittent streams to catch up to the brook.

Chase was all about fishing. Whether I was sitting down or swat-ting bugs away, he was showing off, catching fish after fish. Maybe it was the bait he used or the line, I couldn't tell.

"So, who taught you how to fish?"

"My grandpa and my uncle. We always went. I will have to buy you your own fishing rod."

"Does your mom fish?"

"Nope."

Chase was a mamma's boy.

There was no one else down at the fishing hole. Where the river rushed along, it pooled into a separate little hole we fished out from.

"There are so many bugs out. It's horrible! Do you have any bug spray?"

"No. Sorry, I don't think I do."

He looked over and put down his fishing rod to gather wood. He started to built a fire. It was blazing; and ferociously hot. He kept stoking it until the fire was massive.

"This will keep the bugs away. Well, it helps anyway. Come over here," he said.

The heat burned hot against my face. I stood back and watched the fire. Soon, the smoke signalled the sky for the night to come. I took another step closer to him and he put his arms around me.

I feel the weather changing and I look at the darkening sky. It would be best I follow the channel back down the mountain, stay near the water to take me back home. Under a black canopy, sudden destruction comes. I know the lion is on the prowl, and I should have run.

Everyone tells me he is reckless and to stay away from him. My sun-tanned skin and doll-lit eyes looked like the pride of a golden calf. The darkness used me as a pawn in schemes that I was happy to be a part of. Prone to lust and sinful idolatry, banshees called over and over, *drain out her heart and leave her for dead.*

I thought it had meant something when early on Chase told me he loved me. He came to me and told me, "Here this is for you. It has special meaning. This ring comes from my grandmother, passed down to my mom. It is mine, and I want you to have it."

I look at it and admire how, "it is beautiful."

The next time I saw him, the sun was setting. I was wearing a lovely blue dress. I was not looking for permission for what I wanted to take.

I walked down the winding path and around the corner. The river was fast, rushing wild. I came up to him and took his hands and held them in mine. I gazed deep in his eyes, unafraid. "I want to show you something. I promise, you will never forget."

These thoughts rewind in my mind, fearless through the wind, storms, and long nights.

THIRTEEN
CHEERINESS

The times I resurfaced back into reality was when inner-workings of different strings connected to mine were being pulled. It was as if God allowed them to catch my attention. Terrible news was something that stopped everything, forcing me to look at what was going on. It is a part of the beauty of when lives are interwoven so delicately together. You realize that life is a gift and that we are not the ones in control. God is.

When it came to my family, I thought we were more than just a picture of people who came together one day to capture the moment. Apparently, I was the only one who made mistakes. Things were "my fault". I was the one looked down upon as being "black sheep". At the same time, I was the only one who could admit my shortcomings.

Mom hung the family portrait on the wall. Taking a look at my life was something I avoided doing. But when I looked at the picture, we were all human, with our own struggles, pains, and fear. We all had problems, but it felt like I was the only one willing to admit it because it was so brutally obvious. There was nothing subtle in my mistakes or choices. One thing was for certain though, when one of us hurt, we all hurt and came together. Each one of us had strengths, each one of us had weaknesses, but deep down, we all had love in our hearts, and that matters.

The phone rang.

"Hello?"

"Hi Joy."

"Hi Mom, how are you?"

"Not good. Your dad is in the hospital. He suffered a heart attack."

I gasped, "What? Is he okay?"

Mom paused a moment before answering, "Yes, he is okay."

"Where is he?"

"In town."

"How can I get there?" I was frantic. I had never seen it coming. I did not think I could lose my dad.

"Someone will come to get you."

I sat down in grief. Feeling completely sick.

This time, I hung up the phone and turned to God. Why did this have to happen? Was it my fault? Maybe I was not the closest to my dad, but I loved him. He had always been there. He was not one for emotions. His strong suit was hard work and enduring. Not a man of conversation, so when he did talk, it was important. I had missed out on being apart of life with my entire family. I could not get time back.

I needed to change.

I cried. Feeling the weight of my poor decisions.

"Please God, please. I'm sorry. Please let my dad be okay." I sobbed. "Give me more time to change. I'm not prepared to lose him," I said looking down, choking on my tears; the feeling of a life wasted. The best years of his life and mine. I had been living like a fool and not appreciating all God had given me.

"I never made it right," I cried out with deep remorse. "He has not seen me get out of this mess and turn my life around. Please give me time. If I lose him, I will have such horrible regrets."

I blew my nose and wiped my eyes with a tissue. In that moment of uncertainty, it felt like it was me and God; and I was tender. It felt like God loved me. God cared, and that He had not turned His back on me.

I gathered myself together and got ready to see Dad.

When I walked into the hospital room, nothing prepared me for the moment I saw him lying in bed with wires, tubes, and patches all over his body. I slowly walked in and looked at him. His eyes were soft, steely grey, and a little wet looking. I had never seen my dad so fragile. I was scared.

"How are you feeling, Dad?" I asked, giving him a gentle hug, looking at him like I was seeing him for the first time. I was holding onto the moment. My dad wasn't Superman. He was not indestructible. He was made from dust, and the man he was I did not know. Where had we parted ways? It was so long ago and I took for granted I would get time back.

"I'm doing pretty good. Dr. Vandemere saved my life! He was ready with the Beta Blocker the second I got in the hospital," Dad said smiling.

I was surprised by his cheeriness.

"We will get better. Let's get better together," he said to me. Once again, I was caught off guard and nodded my head in agreement. I felt as vulnerable as Dad.

My sisters and I said our good-byes after the visit, then left his room. It took them less than a minute before they both turned on me.

"This is your fault Dad has had a heart attack," they gushed, "if he dies, it's all your fault!"

The arrows were fiery and shot straight through my wounded heart. The stabbing guilt I already felt was insurmountable. I wanted to get out of there as fast as I could.

My sisters could see the stress I put on my parents. My family was tired of it. They were leading productive lives and I caused the problems. I thought my loving parents were the only ties remaining to practical goodness, and without them, nothing would be left of me.

I would do my hardest to try and quit meth. I felt the preciousness of time and every priority seemed so clear. It was not a hard decision to make. I was done using.

As my dad got better, so did I. I made it an entire month without using. That was a major accomplishment.

As I started to feel my dad's health was returning, I let my guard down. I made the fatal mistake and started using again. I fell out of the loving arms that I belonged to. I had slipped again.

I started to believe that I did not know how to live sober. I would go to rehab, come back home, only to relapse again. I start hanging out with the same friends that I should have stayed far away from. I was rebellious, but not only that, I had a hard heart. Where did that get me? It was always "my way", which was always the "wrong way". I failed every time. I was lost to that world.

I did not know how to change myself in a way that I could be made complete. I did not have the answer to "fix" me. This was a monster that I could not defeat. I did not understand the things that needed to happen in my life. Jesus would fix my brokenness if I went to Him and repented. I was down here and Jesus seemed so far away. The answer to the darkness is the light. Complete freedom in Jesus Christ. I needed light! Lots of it! Light, light, and more light! Jesus Christ is the light! Surely I could see I needed Jesus. Truly, I was so blind!

I felt like a complete failure to my parents, to my sisters, and the kids. I would think to myself, *my dad had a heart attack, and I can't even get clean for longer then a month – pretty pathetic.* The devil was always there to keep me defeated, beating me up over my horrible feelings of failure and relapse. How could I not love my family enough to stay sober? Another problem was that it was my willpower versus the devil. Satan turns things upside down. That is part of the meaning of his name. That is why the satanic symbol is upside down. Jesus Christ crushed him. Praise God.

So, I was off. Reckless, back to the forbidden caves of the dark kingdom, destroying my life and mind. The old familiar hissing of serpents was everywhere, and they did not bother hiding their presence anymore.

I was wearing a dark grey hoodie with skulls all over it. My bleached blonde hair had a tint of orange to it. It looked crimped from the braid I had taken out. Chase was wearing a grey T-shirt. Our skin both looked bleached white against the blackness of our eyes. We both looked off skid row.

We were getting high in his room, and I needed more drugs.

"Can we smoke another bowl?"

"No."

"I feel dope sick. I need to smoke a little more. Then I will be okay."

"No. I'm not smoking another bowl."

"Come on. I'm sick. Please. I need more."

"No. Sorry. I'm not."

He got up and left the room.

The devil suited up and had a malicious temper tantrum. This was displeasing. *It demanded sacrifice.* I had to kill this thing that was festering. The tail had surfaced. It screamed at me through hollow walls that kindled red burning flames. I looked down at my arms. *I didn't care. Why should I? I had nothing,* and I begin to slash.

Blood began to surface. Ouch. I stopped for a moment. The cut was raw and the sting irritated my skin. The flesh on my arm was tender, delicate, and soft. Past scars were still sitting there, like visible train tracks running down my arm. They had not moved, reminding me of a time long ago, when I had been tremendously hurt. I would never cut that deep ever again.

At least I was being a good girlfriend and not causing drama by hounding Chase for drugs. At the time, I didn't know what else to do, and this feeling needed to die. I had to kill it, and I kept slashing. It does not hurt, until the skin opened up. The twist within feels satisfied with the sight of crimson, calming things down. The sacrifice was excepted. The room was quiet – too quiet. I got carried away, and soon there was an overwhelming amount of blood. At least I didn't have to feel the rage of being a phene in pain; it was too intense to handle. Great. I was going to have obvious cuts all over my arms, and I had a job. I didn't need anyone to see. I didn't really want my arms to be covered with more slash scars, so I needed to move to my legs.

Chase walked in the room, and I quickly looked up at him nervous.

"What are you doing?" he asked suspicious, noticing the quiet and not trusting it. He looked down at me, sitting in his closet.

Oh no. I wanted to hide. I felt myself shrivelling up.

"What do you have in your hand?" he asked.

"Nothing," I answered inconspicuous, hiding the blade beneath me. He grabbed for my arm. I was busted. He pulled me up, seeing the blood and cuts.

"What are you doing?" he demanded. His brown eyes searched for reasoning in my madness.

I was a wreck, a complete compromised mess.

"You're trying to kill yourself? You need to leave!" he was furious.

The words shot an arrow right through me, and I stepped back and clutched my heart.

"What? No. I'm not going anywhere." Are you kidding me? Couldn't he see my pain? That I needed drugs?

"Look, I'm fine. I was just trying to take the edge off. Listen to me when I say it is no big deal. I'm sorry. I just need to wrap it up, and I will be fine. I won't do it again."

Chase was upset, "You better never cut yourself again, or I will break up with you. Okay?"

"Ya," I said softly, with my head down, ashamed.

"Okay, I will find you a shirt to wrap your arm up, but maybe you should go to the hospital."

I insisted, "No. I will be okay. I will just use your shirt. I'm sorry. I love you."

"I love you too Joy. You do some stupid things sometimes. You are going to give me a heart attack."

"I will try better. I'm sorry. I was overwhelmed by the sickness, and I didn't know what to do."

"Don't be cutting yourself. I'm serious."

I closed my eyes. "I know. I told you I won't."

I got into bed, feeling bad for what I had done. I hated upsetting him.

"Come here," he said, which made me feel a little better, as if I had some of his forgiveness. I couldn't help but tell him how much I cared about him.

"When you hold me, I feel like someone more than traces of an empty chalk line." He held me closer as I lay my head on his chest and snuggled closely.

I thought to myself time and time again that it was always going to be me and him. The message was clear. When he looked at me, I knew his desires, and he took my hand.

"Feel my heart beating." I could hear it pounding, loud and fast. Woe. I didn't realize how much that incident affected him. Maybe he really did care.

"Look at me. Look in my eyes."

And I looked into his eyes, and they took me in deep.

FOURTEEN
THE ONE

"I hate you!" I screamed at him, yelling with all my fury. I was lunatic mad. Raging crazy, planning to knock him out. I had found out that Chase had cheated on me. I listened to his voicemail messages and heard the sound of sweetness oozing, and it wasn't from me.

I stormed into his sister's trailer, burst right in there. He was standing there in the kitchen and I pounced right for him.

"You jerk!"

"What did I do?" he asked, looking up at me.

I had all the evidence I needed.

I glared right at him and punched him hard as I could, right in the eye. Hopefully that would slap the confusion out of his head. He did not see it coming. He was cooking rice on the stove. I grabbed his prized possession Blue-Jays hat, and threw it on the element, starting it on fire. He grabbed his hat and put it under water.

I know you cheated on me! "Oh, Chase! Oh, Chase!" I glared at him with stabbing daggers in my eyes, imitating the voice I had heard over his phone.

He came up to me holding his eye, "Babe! You just sucker punched me! I can't believe you did that!"

"It's over. I never want to talk to you ever again!"

I was pissed off and kicked a small hole in the wall of the trailer as I stormed out of there. I got into my blue Honda Civic and floored it. I hated him. What a chronic liar.

He showed up a few days later with a black eye and an apology. I was done.

The fights were a constant strain – like a loud bee or a fly that goes buzz-buzz trapped inside your car window in the heat of the summer day. You just wish it would die already or figure a way out, so you wouldn't have to listen to it keep hitting itself against the wind shield, feeling trapped, trying to get out.

Over at my place, we were standing in the kitchen talking.

"You just talk down to me. You're rude and talk to me like I'm not good enough." I said, tired and defeated.

"I'm sorry. I know I can be a jerk," he said.

"You think everything I do is unimportant, and you're never happy, or even try to be nice. I can't take anymore."

"Things will change."

"Ya, right. I have endured as much as I can. I tried to hang in to make it work, but mentally and emotionally I just feel like you are ruining me. I'm at the end of all I can handle."

"I'm sorry. I will make it up to you."

"You can't. All we do is fight. Every time we go fishing together you complain the entire time. I am starting to hate fishing now." I was deeply hurt.

"Babe. I'm sorry," he says sweetly.

"You are ruining my life. I don't like seeing stars spinning around my head when you punch me. It scares me. You dropped me hard."

He tries to calm me, "I will be better, I promise. I love you. I'm sorry about that. I'm a total jerk."

"You cheated on me..."

"No, I never," he grinned, laughing it all off.

"Dude, I heard you rented a hotel room right across from my work," I said, rolling my eyes at him. "How ignorant. That is super messed up. That is sick you know."

He sounded surprised, "where'd you hear that?"

"Who cares where I heard it?" I looked at him.

He tried to give me a hug, but I'm guarded. I do not want to hope in his lies, and I left the room.

There was no point in arguing him or fighting back.

I tried to hit him with my car once, but he dodged it like a wild bullet. He was lucky. There was no stopping him. I truly wanted to hospitalize him. Than I would not have to worry. He needed help in settling down. And I thought that might be the only way.

I could see I was missing out on so much more. I lived for a bag of dope that had no meaning. What I was truly longing for was to be normal, which felt more like an honest privilege. People had no clue how blessed they were to not go down the path I had dug. It is life ruining, exhausting, and very lonely. The longer you are trapped, the more hopeless you feel. But hopelessness is a lie. You are not hopeless at all. No matter how low or bad you feel, that is not the truth. It is a lie. You might not understand it. But God is a God of awe, mystery, and power. He makes things right.

Driving in my car, listening to the radio play. The humble DJ had charm that endeared one, reminding me of a tweety bird that was in high spirits; always chirping away.

I noticed people walking down the sidewalk. How wonderful normal people's lives must be. What I wanted was a jumbo, life-sized cereal box of hope that I could get off these drugs that controlled me. I needed a different road. I was not asking for much. I wanted love. True love. And sobriety. I wanted more. I wanted to live again. I wanted to be normal.

I approached the stop light and waiting for the green. The breeze was gently blowing, when a lightly coloured feather came floating down and came to rest on my windshield. It reminded me of the gold dusted feather. It drifted with the wind, always passing but never stopping. Just maybe, these feathers belonged to guardian angels who watched over us.

It was rare to find loyalty. Maybe it was timing, maybe it was corruption, or maybe that was just the limelight of misdirected thoughts that visited my mind. It was like shaping something that was special to me, just to break me. Mom gave me a brown jewellery box to hold my treasures. Two worlds with different meanings, each passed down, like the ring I once wore from Chase. My dad had told me to give it back to him. I did not want to, but for once I listened.

A few months later of this on-again-off-again sledge-hammer romance, I was over at Chase's place, sitting on his bed. My back was against the wall, and I was telling him about the tough morning I had. My boss, Noreen, had been diagnosed with lung cancer, and it took her quickly. It was a tremendous loss. I was saddened at my pathetic condition. Her daughter Rita had come in the store that morning. It was a gloomy Sunday, maybe after 6:30 a.m. They had closed up the UFA Petroleum store and everyone went home.

"I'm sorry, babe. Well, maybe now is a good time that you should go back to rehab?" he suggested.

I sat there and continued to blow my nose. I had already been to rehab; Aventa, and GP.

"Well, my parents are on my case, telling me to go. I will go if you go," I answered...

"I got a job. I will go eventually," was his defence.

"I don't want to go without you," I sighed, feeling like it was pointless, "do you got a bowl to smoke?"

"Yes." He got up, opened his sock drawer, and pulled out his pipe.

CLEAVE TO JESUS CHRIST

"Okay, don't burn the bottom black."

"Well, burn it for me then." He grabbed the lighter.

"I remember the nicest thing you ever said to me. Do you remember what it was?"

"Nope. What was it?"

"You said to me, 'I sure lucked out when I met you.' That was so nice. I won't ever let you forget it," I said, cheering up a bit.

"I love you. It will all be okay."

I looked over at the window, feeling melancholy. My eyes closed like heavy shutters, and I started dreaming about Chase. I was falling fast, and it was an arduous landing. *He winked at me, and it made me smile. He held my heart with his bare hands and stared at it intently, examining how it beat. He took one step back and twisted it right in front of me. I clasped the hole inside my chest. I cried out, "Stop!" He took another step back and grinned, watching the effect he had on me. I was begging on my knees, crying for mercy. He started squeezing with all his might. Blood was squirting out, and he was covered in it. He knelt down and put my twisted heart back inside my chest and promised me, "It still works, except the beat may be a little off." He chuckled, patting me on the head. I looked up at him, shaking my head.* I woke up suddenly.

"Chase, I got a headache."

"Ya." He was not paying attention; he was playing video games.

"Do you have any Tylenol?"

"Ya, I got some in my fishing bag." he motioned to his black bag that was sitting inside his closet. I got up off the bed. I reached over for his bag and unzipped the front pocket. I looked inside and rummaged around. I was gutted by what I found.

"Dude. Whose are these?" Chase looked over at me curiously. I pulled out a pair of ladies' underwear.

He didn't know what to say.

"Um," he stammered.

My blush was fever hot, and tears streamed down my face.

"Joy. Please calm down."

"Calm down? I think you need to get rid of them. I got to go." My mind was frazzled. Although, I was not surprised at the things he did anymore. I had come to expect them.

I opened his brown bedroom door and put on my shoes. They were sitting by the front door. I didn't know where to go, but I got in my car and took off down to the river.

I walked along the water bank. The water was high. The sky was grey, and I didn't know what to do anymore. I looked up. I'm not sure what made me decide to hike up the steep embankment. Half way up, I was drenched in sweat, yet I felt drought in the depths of my soul. My hands were all cut up from the jagged rocks. I wished I had something to drink. I was so thirsty. I rested for a few moments then kept going. Finally, I made it to the top.

I was exhausted and already dreaded that I would have to go all the way back down. I sat on the edge of the cliff, looking at the steep drop. In between thorns and prickles from dead rose brushes, the grass was more like broken-looking straw – long, white, and lifeless. The river that meant so much to me was pulling me under its current. My sense of belonging to the beauty of the river had long drowned.

I wiped the tears from eyes and looked intently at the sky. It looked as dreary as I felt, yet still so captivating. In my heart, I felt like I was sitting there, facing God.

"I am in an awful place here God." And I broke down in gut wrenching tears. *Why did I have to throw my life away? My life sucks. Why does life have to be so hard?* I hung my head defeated. I sat in that condition for hours. I was the one who made all my own mistakes. I had thrown my life away. I had been so blind. I knew where it led: a cemetery of dead bones. Life kept knocking me down, and I felt my ability to keep getting back up was lessening every time. The sun started to set, and I picked myself up, and headed back down.

It was a lie to believe no one cared or to think I was alone. God truly cares about all our hurts and pain. I remembered it was I who had closed the door and shut God out of my life. Instead I let the world in.

> Those who are well have no need of a physician, but those who are sick. But go and learn what this means: *I desire mercy and not sacrifice.* For I did not come to call the righteous, but sinners, to repentance. Matthew 9:12-13

> "For the Son of Man has come to save that which was lost. What do you think? If a man has a hundred sheep, and one of them goes astray, does he not leave the ninety-nine and go to the mountains to seek the one that is straying? And if he should find it, assuredly, I say to you, he rejoices more over that sheep than over ninety-nine that did not go astray. Even so it is not the will of your Father who is in heaven that one of these little ones should perish." Matthew 18:10-14

When I went back home, Chase was there, waiting to talk to me.

"I'm sorry, Joy," slowly he started spinning his web.

"It's over." I told him plainly. "Does it occur to you that I can't handle this?"

"Joy, I love you," he lied.

"No. I can't even risk being hurt anymore. I'm rented. I don't want to do this anymore. Why should I have to?"

"Babe, come on. Things will be better. I love you."

He grabbed me and gave me a hug. But I could not stay in those arms, where I wanted to be.

"You don't love me though! Last week you told me I should kill myself. You are ruining me. There is nothing left. I'm exhausted. Go be with whoever you want. I don't care anymore. Just leave me alone."

"No. I did not mean it. I am sorry. I won't leave you."

Three months passed.

FIFTEEN
FINISH HER OFF!

The red and blue night sirens were becoming something of a grab and go, but not tonight. Chase had been telling me how much he loved me all night long. He left, and later on, I got ready to pick him up to go fishing.

I drove over to Lacy's place down the pot-holed ridge road. The road was notorious for being so littered with pot-holes, even if you swerved, you couldn't miss hitting one. It was so neglected that it made the newspaper. Even after all the constant complaints from tenants, it still never got paved. It was annoying to everyone who was stuck living there and excruciatingly hard on vehicles.

I was not allowed over at Ms. Lacy's trailer. Even after I plastered the hole I had made. She did not want any damage done to her trailer. Lacy came storming out of the trailer when I pulled up.

"You need to leave. Chase *hates* you!"

Why should I be surprised? So much drama. But it hurt, obviously because I loved him. What was she talking about? Even being high couldn't kill the pain. Chase took my emotions up and then down. Love than hate. At least I could always blame my misery on him. Instead of being responsible for my own choices.

"I'm not leaving."

I needed to understand what was going on.

"He is my boyfriend and I want to talk to him." I didn't care what any one thought. I did not think I was being irrational. In fact, I was being calm. I thought it was fair enough that I wanted to talk to him. I didn't think I was the one freaking out here. I was worried sick in my driver seat, not budging, until he decided to be a man and come talk to me. "I just know he is going to go cheat on me. I just need to talk to him."

"I'm calling the police if you do not leave!" she screamed infuriated at me and turned back inside. I sat waiting in my car. I was getting pissed off. I honked my horn. Big deal. It was the middle of the day. I had not slept in a few days. That was half of the problem and caring about Chase was the rest. Clarity in any of this was not going to happen until I talked to him. Twenty minutes passed and the police showed up.

"What is going on?" the cop asked, setting me gently in his cruiser. The back-seat leather felt tight in a big, cold space of emptiness.

"What did I do? I never did anything wrong!"

Why was this happening? I hated Chase! This was all his fault!

The cop got in the car. "Look, they were the party that called, so I have to take you in. You caused the disturbance by honking your horn and not leaving."

"Are you serious? It is the middle of the day? I went to ask my boyfriend to go fishing, that's it! This is not making any sense. He is the one with the warrant for arrest, and I'm going to jail?"

"I was being nice. I didn't handcuff you or want to embarrass you."

We pulled up to the station and got out. He took me in, fingerprinted me, and then put me in the cell. All I could think about was how much I hated Chase for allowing this to happen. Truly I had no value. If this was how Chase felt about me, then what was hate?

Officially, I had sunk into the depths of mire. This was the next bottom. I had never been so low. This had a brute hold that was not going to give. It pushed me into madness, right off the edge. I may had done plenty things to deserve this, but not today. I would never forgive him.

I looked around the room. Being there made me feel absolutely horrible inside. I was exhausted. I closed my eyes, worn-out, trying to escape.

A gentle tapping on the iron bars startled me. The police told me, "it is time to go." And he released me. I had been through the ringer. I was done being plowed over. I guarantee you, I was not the same person when I left jail that day.

I picked up my car with all my hatred reserved for Chase. No, I loathed him. Why didn't he just leave me alone? Evil escorted me home that day. I was wearing the heaviest cloak. By the time I was home, I had surpassed rage. I was so hurt and broken, I was at death's door.

I did not just accidentally "stumble" my way into this place. This is what I chose. It was years of dedication to sin and bad choices. I did not realize that I was sitting in the waiting room of suicide. Now, death imposed itself on me, telling me, *it is your turn*. My clock was slowly winding down. The wait was not on evil; the wait was on me. How long did they have to keep attacking me before they broke my will and pushed me over the edge?

For days I lay in my bed.

I was in a catatonic state, past exhaustion and failure; at the highest point of vulnerability. I was under the spell of evil, and it could tell me anything it wanted. The darkness devoured my mind and had me subjugated under its control. I was its hostage. I listened to it declare my last rights for me.

I had nothing! I had nothing to live for!

You're all alone again. Don't you think you have had enough?

Your n-o-t-h-i-n-g – no one loves you!

I was naked. I don't remember taking off my clothes.

When what you see makes you sad.

What you have makes you sad.

What you do makes you sad.

What you love makes you sad.

What you could have had makes you sad.

Who you should have been makes you sad...

I took a turn for the worse.

"Stop it! Fine!"

It was too intense. It was too much! I gave up.

"Fine. Have it your way! Just give me peace!"

I got off my bed, looking for a way out.

I looked around my room and saw a big metal hook. I used it to hang my bike up in the ceiling. I grabbed a chair and put it on my bed. I stood on it. It was wobbly. I held my balance, lightly knocked, found a stud, and screwed the hook in. Pride chimed in...

It's going great.

The mood shifted as I obeyed. As long as I listened to the principalities of the darkness, they backed off. At this point, they were squealing in glee. They had gathered around me, like at a funeral service when you stand around the casket as it is lowered down into the earth. Evil was united, ready to welcome my soul to hell for eternal damnation. Soon, the torture would all be just the beginning, not ending.

I turned the hook round and round, until it was too hard to turn. I got my pliers to finish the project.

You're doing such a great job! Don't you feel better? Soon you will have eternal peace!

Oh great! Finally.

Feel satisfaction that you could so easily find a stud in the ceiling. After all those tweak projects. See? It finally paid off, and no one can take that away from you.

I looked around, saw a luggage strap, and picked it up.

I sat down on my bed, one last time. I felt utter hopelessness. This is what absolute rock bottom feels like. I had hit it. I needed peace. I looked at the strap in my hands. I was about to take my life. Was I sure? I felt such sorrow. Tears tenderly rolled down my cheeks. I was in a daze. No clarity. I had not thought to write a goodbye letter. Once again, the torment started to bully me. My mind was crushed like napalm, a force too traumatic for me to endure. I was ready to follow it. I stood up and stepped up on the chair.

See if you can go through with it. The lies and the pain, they are just too much. You are broken. There is no hope! Just put your head in. Try it. See how it fits. Besides...it is not hard to pull yourself out of the noose, and you can always change your min. You're a strong girl... remember that. You are so brave! No one understands what you have to go through!

I agreed with that, so I made the next move.

I stood on the wobbling chair.

No sense, truth, reason, or logic, just darkness that loomed, waiting for me to step out. I remember these last words, *"what a sad way to end it."* This is it.

I stuck my head in the noose.

No turning back. I strung myself up in defeated torment. I kicked the chair out from underneath my feet. Having no thought, except for the moment.

SIXTEEN

MY DELIVERER!

"My sheep hear My voice, and I know them, and they follow Me. And I give them eternal life, and they shall never perish; neither shall anyone snatch them out of My hand. My Father, who has given them to Me, is greater than all; and no one is able to snatch them out of My Father's hand. I and My Father are one." John 10:27-29

It was dead silent in the room. The peace was gentle and calm. I felt in a daze. I looked up. The strap had broken –and my neck hadn't. I was unharmed. I was in shock. What had I just done?

I sat up, bewildered in amazement. The fog had lifted. It was so still in the room – I felt the perfect peace that I was ready to die for. All the torment that would not subside had been silenced by the power of God. Evil was sucked out of the room the moment I stepped off the chair. God heard my cry. It came into His very ears. My help comes from The Lord. Psalm 121

Jesus Christ had showed up, intercepted on my behalf, thwarting the plans of the enemy. I felt sealed to Jesus Christ. He was there by my side. Not even in my darkest moment was I ever alone.

I thought back to a time long ago, the King, and the complete radiance of His light. He possesses kindness that is *so* tender, and his greatest desire is to save a lost soul.

I needed to get out of my bedroom and go to my mom's.

God be the glory! Thank you, Jesus. I exalt you. Thank you for saving me.

I get dressed and drove to my parents' house. I need to get off drugs, like today. I sobbed when I told Mom. And once again, Jesus was there by my side. His peace was like a wave that washed over me. He held me still, and troubles felt so distant. I felt His love. My tears stopped. The Father wiped them away. It felt so pure. I sat there feeling His comfort, protection, and stillness. I felt God hold me.

My parents had put their trust and hope in God. They depended on Him to save me. The hardest thing my mom had to do was step aside and let God have me. It was the only way my addiction would not destroy her. She was learning to trust God and learning to live by faith, not by what she could see, but by what God promised her. God kept protecting me, delivering me out of the snares of death.

The night eventually passed. I hung around my parents' house as long as I could, but I had a job and had to go to work. I was trying my hardest to stay clean, but by day three, I could not function at work sober. I was a complete wreck. And I was over the sheer cliffs of insanity. My body was stiff, unable to move. Everyone thought I was really strung out, but it was the opposite. I was so dope sick. I was fighting for my life with all I had to escape death's grip. I was weak. Maybe I was never meant to be strong. Maybe I was truly meant to rely on God's strength.

Months later, I drove over to my dealer's house and opened her gate. There were puppies running around – beautiful red-nosed pit bulls, and I went inside to talk to Cassie.

I had met Cassie when I was clean, right before I started dating Chase. I ran into Cassie at the Old Hotel, in the bar. She worked at the coat check. Her glowing confidence drew me in immediately. The

Cadillac lure in her eyes invigorated charm, and her red hair warned "temper temper".

"Hey," I say to her. I was sober and she was lit, and I missed the feeling. I usually avoided places where I ran into users, and I handed her my jacket.

She smiled, "hey, here's the number for your coat. Just bring me the paper when you need your coat back."

Did she remember me from high school? She was a year older. I wondered what happened along her lines of life. I took the paper from her. Shortly afterwards, I showed up at her door, asking for drugs. She told me, "get lost." A couple years later, the dust finally settled.

"Hey Cassie. How's it going? Are those your puppies?"

I stood in her bedroom. Her bed had clothes on it. It was in the middle of her room and Sharon was sitting on it.

"Hey Joy, how's it going?" Sharon asked pleasantly.

"Good, how about you?"

"Well, I'm doing good. Those puppies are so cute."

"Yep, they are mine," Cassie answered me with a grin, and looked up from going through her clothes.

Cassie, Sharon, and I were all looking for answers. It was the bad boys showing up who were the ones we had to watch out for. They came around, beating our doors down until we let them in. Today there was no boys, just wonderful four-legged friends.

"Hey, are you selling those puppies? Can I buy one from you?"

"They are eating me out of house and home. Yes, they are for sale, $250," Cassie said.

"Well, I don't have that much. Can I make payments to you every time I get paid?" I asked hopeful. Maybe having a dog would do me some good.

"Sure," she smiled at me.

"Okay, I'm going to go look and see which one I want!"

The one that caught my eye was brown and white. She was the runt and reminded me of Bambi. I took her with me over to Tyler's house, trying to come up with the perfect name. Tyler had blonde hair and was a year younger than me. We used together. He had the craziest girlfriend I ever met. Luckily, she was not home. We sat around for hours, tossing out names.

"Call her Daisy." Tyler suggested, as he sat there with his guitar.

"No. I already had a dog called that before. Besides, she is brown."

"How about Lily?"

"No, that does not suit."

"Um, Mars?"

"Na. It has to be perfect."

"How about Pluto? Jet? Diesel..."

"Diesel? Hmmn. That reminds me of a special song."

"Sandman?" he smiled.

"How about... Nova. Her name is Nova."

"Ya. Nova is a great name."

"Thanks Tyler."

I moved into a different place with Nova and Chase ended up moving in too. It was drama central. When pay day hit, I needed to find him. I went up town and found him sitting at the slot machines. I pulled him out of the bar and it turned into an argument outside in the parking lot. He was unbelievable. He conspired to gamble his entire paycheck away in a single sitting. I wanted to have his fair share of the rent money before it was gone within the hour.

"Please, give me some rent money. Or you will spend it all."

"I'm only giving you $100. I will give you the rest later."

"Dude, no you won't. I know you. You will spend it all."

"You are not getting all of it."

"Why not?"

"I will give it all to you later."

"No you won't. Look, I don't care what you do. Just please give me some rent money."

I agonized, and he was stubborn.

"No. I will give it to you later."

We were startled by two vehicles pulling up abrasively. Six good looking men opened the truck doors and streamed out. They had badges and took assertion around us.

The chief officer stood across from us, he came in his own vehicle.

"You guys are being loud."

I stared at him, stunned.

Chase was nervous. He had left a huge bruise on my upper leg from throwing a rock at me. I wanted Chase to feel the heat. The bruise was huge. It had been a painful. I had on a dress, and I made sure that officer took notice.

"Do you want to press charges?" he asked.

"No." I answered.

And Chase took off, before he could get in trouble.

Tall, dark and handsome asked me the quick-fire questions. My mind was in a whirlwind. His questions tripped me up.

"How old are you?"

I did not know. I was twenty-eight. Then realized shamefully, "thirty-two."

Where had the time gone?

"Do you want help?"

The question reverberated down into my consciousness. It sent shock waves into my shredded soul. I stood before them dead. Do I want help? With all the darkness that consumed my life, suddenly a light shined bright, directly on me. Their questions triggered hope. A needed a reminder that a complete stranger could care. It touched my heart. God used the experience to spark a search and rescue. I needed answers. Not solutions the world held, but for the truth that was buried deep. No matter how many holes I dug with the enemy, I still had faith. And I had to find it.

"Yes." I nodded.

"There is a meeting Tuesday night. It is for Violence Prevention. Ask for Rita."

"Okay," I answered quick and left. I had to go check on Nova. Praise God. He was above it all.

Tuesday night was sure to be filled with all sorts of surprises. The same flashy vehicles drove around town. I pulled up and parked my car. There were vehicles parked on both sides of the street. Two buildings faced one another. In both buildings the lights were on.

I got out of my car and walked into the meeting. I asked for Rita right away. I was surprised. Rita was Noreen's daughter. She made me feel welcome. Rita was warm and lovely, with a pretty woman laugh. Her smile glowed from her eyes, and I clicked with her right away. She is a woman on a mission to be used for God. As the evening progressed, I was a little confused. Why were they were not discussing anything about violence prevention? They acted like they were from a different planet. One guy was far out and radical. He had long blonde hair. He jumped up on the chairs and moved all over the room. He made me nervous; and he was loud. His name was John; a Son of The Thunder. He was talking about Jesus Christ.

I started asking some questions. And that is when I realized, I had walked into the wrong building. The complete wrong meeting. Something else was going on Tuesday nights in Drayton Valley. Serious recovery meetings at the Life Church. It happened to be across the street from the Violence Prevention meeting. Both meetings started at 7 pm. I found out that both meetings were being run by ladies named "Rita". I shook my head and smiled to myself when I left. That was interesting for sure.

After the meeting I went over to Tyler's place.

"Knock knock."

"Hey, come in."

"Hey, how's it going?"

"Pretty good. Just chillin, playing my guitar."

"Ya, I seen Chase up town. I don't think he came home last night."

"Nope. I think he was with Helena. Did you hear about it?"

"Shucks no, and I don't care."

"Well, last night, I think they were down at the diamonds, they slept together in the shack."

I gasped, charged up. "No Way! Are you serious? I hate him. Do you have any gas? Let's go burn it down when it gets dark out."

"You serious? You want to burn it?"

"Ya. I want to torch it!" I exclaimed. My blood was boiling. That shack needed to be destroyed.

"I need to wear black. What you got?"

"Um, check in my closet."

I got up and rummaged through bags of clothes and started to get dressed.

"How do I look?"

"Great."

"Are you going to help?"

"Ya, of course."

"Let's go. We can leave Nova in the truck."

Tyler got dressed. It was past night fall. We drove by and staked the place out. Then pulled back around and parked.

"Give me the gas. Let's go."

"Uh, I don't got gas, I got a bottle of lighter fluid."

"Will that work? Man, I wish we had kerosene."

"It should work." Tyler nodded.

We hopped out and went into the old abandoned building. We walked up the concrete steps. Sure enough, there was a blanket, candle, and a pillow. All I saw were kindling flames in my eyes.

"Let's burn it!"

We doused the blanket, walls, and lit a cloth on fire. We threw it on the lighter fluid and took off.

We saw flames shooting out. It was a rainy cold night, and we went back to Tyler's to watch.

Sure enough, in his high-rise apartment, the smoke billowed up in the night sky. We watched out the window with his binoculars. I could not wait until Chase discovered his hide out love shack burned down to the ground. I thought with some smug satisfaction. It was war.

"I'm going to take Nova and go home."

"See you tomorrow."

"Ya. See you."

The next day, Nova and I went down to the river. While we were there, an ominous feeling came over me. I looked around, over at the trees. There were tall pine's all along the bank. Was someone lurking? My senses were heightened. I had a strong sense of *urgency* come over me. I needed to pack up and get out of there, fast. My life was not safe. I needed to get to higher ground immediately. A very dark threatening presence was upon me, intensely pressing hard to get my soul and finish off the job. I felt it keenly. I needed to start making changes soon. The savour of death was upon me. I was running out of time, fast.

On my way back into town, I drove past the shack. I felt spurned that the building still stood, undefeated against my fury. I was expecting a giant ruin of ash and rubble. Oh, what morning glory. It was definitely in my best interest that the building still stood. It would have been a frightening and sickening sight. I would have felt so guilty. Surely, I would not have caused such destruction from my very precious hands. Even though I hated the shack, I let go of the pretension. I just will not drive by it. I was thankful. And I gave Tyler the news.

Chase tried rehab again, and I waited for him. When Chase got home, he did not call me. I found out a few weeks later that he had a new girlfriend, and I was crushed. Whatever. He could keep his new girlfriend. I did not need him anyway.

Chase and his new girlfriend did not last long. And our fighting possibilities and long shots were over. The police come and took him out of my life. And finally, that was the end of us.

There was no good reason for him to come back around. Handing out chances would be like allowing him to take a knife and stab me repeatedly in the heart. It gets weary. Why people treat others that way, I don't know. I looked at what my own hands were holding – a knife that was smothered in blood. The handle was carved from ivory and held a sharp silver blade. I knew full well I was the furthest thing from innocent. At times I could feel such rage. I had caused my family and others such cruel pain. Living with regret can't change a thing.

A thirst for blood with vexing reasoning. Our earthly atonement's will never ever satisfy. Only the blood of Jesus Christ that was shed for all. It satisfied the wrath of God. It is enough to pacify all the anger in the world. Move on and forgive. For if you forgive men their trespasses, your heavenly Father will also forgive you. But if you do not forgive men their trespasses, neither will your Father forgive your trespasses. Matthew 6:14

I knew Chase and I would eventually break up, but nothing ever prepares you for when it actually happens. Now, all that was left was when he visited me in my nightmares instead of being in my dreams. I carried on without carrying on at all, and the last thing I needed was him. I put his things in my trunk for the thrift store. It looked so empty with his things gone. It was as empty as what I felt standing in that room with him away. His things were still in my trunk, and although it felt like forever since he had been a big part of me, feelings don't suddenly stop just because someone is gone.

I walked along that evening. The rain was falling down, and the thunder was gently booming. It had been a long time since I had seen lightning light up the sky, and I danced a little in the rain. The river was like my second home, although I would have liked to make it my first. I took a chance going back to a place that was filled with painful memories. No matter how many times I went down there, Chase never was. I tried my best not to think on those times or that place, but sometimes I had the urge.

When the pull was strong and the river was raging, I found my way back down there. I walked the dirt road and then made a turn into the bush, only to find the old path we used to walk had grown over with weeds, grass, and logs. I came walking around the corner, like I had done a thousand times before. But this time, my surroundings were completely different. It now looked more like a Promised Land.

I looked up at the bright blue sky, and I had to declare, "Wow, God. I'm impressed." God was there already, waiting for me. I was blown away. I had never seen so many mustard seed plants in my life! They were amazingly tall and hearty. They stretched along the bank, encompassing the trees, and in between the rocks. God had every inch of that bank covered, in the heights and the depths. I do not know where the seed had sprung from, and it did not matter. God speaks to us, if we only have the eyes, ears, and heart to receive it. We have an amazing God. It spoke volumes to me. When I walk into my future, God will be waiting for me to get there. Maybe today evil is present but learn how to master it. In the end, only God will remain. The entire scene reminded me of a promise: if you have faith the size of a mustard seed, you will say to this mountain, "Move from here to there," and it will move; and nothing will be impossible for you. Matthew 17:21 And what remained at the river bank was entirely in God's hands.

SEVENTEEN
THE GOOD SHEPARD

My parents struggled with my addiction. They thought it would be best to have nothing to do with me. It killed them to see me deteriorate. They prayed for me everyday. The road was getting weary for my dad, who was working outside one day. He was upset and asked, "God, why aren't you doing anything to help Joy in her situation?" God never said anything but answered him a few months later.

Day by day, the temperature slowly dropped, then plummeted. I kept staring up for answers. It turned into a white chilly winter, like every other one. A little bit of snowboarding, which I'm not great at. The wind was blowing cold. It's screaming howled outside my trailer. I did my best to keep Nova tucked in a warm cozy room with soft swaddling blankets especially for her comfort. Oh how I loved Nova so dearly. She was always by my side. My bed room was the third door down the trailer hallway. I had stapled bed sheets to my ceiling that draped lovingly down around my bed.

I sat on my bed, looking outside my window, retreating past the constellations and beyond the moon. I often looked up at the sky. I was trying to see what was underneath that sheet of black night sky. I was searching intently for something more. What was going on with the lights? Were they stars? No, they looked too big to be stars. Were they satellites in orbit? Or space stations that I knew nothing about? No matter how much I pondered, the answers remained a question to me. The drama with Chase was over. I actually had enough silence to think about something else rather than fights or constant stress. I searched for questions about life and my purpose, and tears filled up my eyes again. Life did not feel very good. Could that night sky bring me any truth as I looked to what was behind it, holding all the answers?

The pain I carried was making me ready to break apart. Maybe it was because I had failed every attempt I had made to get clean before, I just had given up on thinking I ever could. What was I living for in my life? What had been so important was now lost to me. I stopped in quiet, not expecting clarity, and in the serenity of the moment, I heard a whisper calling me.

"Come..." I heard it so softly. I was teary-eyed and sombre, and the only way to describe how I was feeling was completely lost.

"Come...come..."

It was slow and deliberate. I was in awe of the essence of it. The voice was like the wind, and it hushed again softly. I was amazed; it was the Holy Spirit. It was important that I acknowledged that I heard it. The Spirit was moving in my life, and I could bet on it. It meant everything to me.

"I want to come, but I can't. I'm so hooked on drugs. They are so powerful. I can't get off them," I answered, sobbing.

There was no denying it. Instantly, I knew the Truth: that the sheep hear His voice. John 10:3

The Shepard looks for His lost sheep, and if one is missing, does He not leave the ninety-nine to go find it? Matthew 18:12

The Word was talking to me. The Bible is literally true. Hearing His call made me believe that I still belonged to God. In my failures, God still loved me; and His arms were open wide, ready to carry me back home to safety. There was hope. It was not to late. I felt something stirring in the room. Maybe I was lost, but I *could* be found. In my pain, I was starting to really look to God. And hope was more then just a powerful feeling, but the truth.

I stayed awake, staring out the window, thinking of the wonder and love of God. Between tired eyes and sought thoughts, I closed my eyes and drifted off to sleep; believing tomorrow did hold purpose and a chance for me.

I woke up excited! Indeed, I had slept the night and let the truth sink down into my ears. Could there be a light glowing in such a dim future as mine? Yep! I'm a sheep. That was my hope! That was all I needed to be. It was boiling down to a calling from the Holy Spirit and a scripture verse that took on such a special meaning in my life. What wonderful news! I had definitely not flown off the radar of God's love.

I needed that love to escape my sickness – for this condition that holds no "common cure". They say it is a disease, you know. It is a sickness you are born with and that you will have to live with forever, for the rest of your God-given, natural life. Well, I didn't care what the experts say. I heard the Holy Spirit calling this little lost sheep. That was all I needed to know. If God was still my Shepard, then my identity was not lost. The Shepard is where and how I could find myself. I just had to hang in there and keep looking and calling for Jesus Christ.

I did not have a clue what was in the works for me or my dire situation. In fact, I had no clue of the magnitude of what waited on the horizon. I started a series of attempts to stop using. Plus, I did not have much money, so the lack of drugs was taking an even worse mental toll. I could make it three days. I wanted that peace again. I always believed that God would save me one day. I knew God was the only way, and I really needed His help. I always felt safe when I went to Him, like He would always be there for me.

I WILL BE A REFUGE FOR THE OPPRESSED, A REFUGE IN TIMES OF
TROUBLE, THOSE WHO KNOW MY NAME WILL PUT THEIR TRUST
IN ME. I HAVE NOT FORSAKEN THOSE WHO SEEK ME. Psalm 9:9-10

That sure sounded simple enough to me. I could never run from this
drug; it would always find me. Maybe I could temporally escape, but it
would always wait patiently for the opportune moment to hit.

Weeks later I sat on my bed, feeling terrible. Oppression was telling
me, *life was hopeless and empty.* It was just pain, so what was the point?
Although suicide tried to insist it was my next of kin, I knew at least to
run from it. I had no one else to turn to, and I was drained.

I made the best decision of my life, when I got up off my little bed,
and humbly dropped to my knees. I started shaking. I guess my emotions and life just broke right down. I had a lifetime of pain on those
knees and the tears – oh, the tears I cried. I grasp difficulty finding the
proper words to convey any of it. I was a broken human being. This
pain was coming from a dead soul that was crying out in distress to God
to make it live again. "Lord Jesus. I am so sorry. Please Lord. Please," I
sobbed, begging out to Him. "I need You Lord. Please. Forgive me."
It was earth-shatter pleading. I surrendered everything. I was on my
knees until I was done begging. My legs had fallen asleep under me.
It hurt for me to get up. I finished hours later, when I had no tears left
within me. I was exhausted, then lay down on my bed and fell to sleep.

I called on Your name, O Lord, from the lowest pit. You
have heard my voice: Do not hide Your ear from my sighing,
from my cry for help." You drew near on the day I called
on You and said, "Do not fear!" Lamentations 3: 55

After a good night's sleep, I felt better. I would really try my very best to go a few days off dope, but by the end of those days, I was high and powerless over the addiction.

I thought about the ex-boyfriend in jail and what time I had wasted on him. I thought about my family and how I had needed a home to go to, but they turned me away. I thought about how I had no job, and how no one would hire me. I was broke, had no food in my fridge, and no one cared. I had wasted the first half of my childhood thinking I did not measure up to the world's standards, and the second half being a complete failure. Back down on my knees, I went in utter misery and pain.

This was another major cry of repentance to God. Inside, I understood that I needed to talk to God and to see this thing through. I needed for Him to hear me, to notice me, to do something – whether it be putting me out of my misery or being my All again. I could not keep going on like this. I wanted out.

"Please...God!" I agonized. "Help me get off these drugs! I'm so sorry, please..." I cried deeply, helplessly on my knees. I felt heartbreak that is indescribable. I cried, screaming out in pain from every corridor within my soul. I needed God in every way possible. There was no other way out, except to ask Thee Most High, the Lord Himself for His personal help.

"Please Lord, I need You, help me," I groaned from my soul, "please, take this from me. I'm so sorry, Lord," I continued, gushing out bucket after bucket of tears.

"Please. Forgive me. Please, Lord. I need You. Lord, please. I need Your help, Lord," I paused helplessly and choked on my tears. "Please, I'm sorry. I don't want to live like this anymore."

I stammered through the words, through the sin, through the nothingness I had become. I had given my soul over to evil. I had made the biggest mistake of my life, and I was there to plead for my soul back! The night took a toll. I was exhausted from being hunched over and begging. I had left it all on the floor. I got up and lay down on my little bed, closed my eyes, and went to sleep. In that little bedroom, I gave my life, my hurts, pain, and failures over to a Faithful and Loving God.

Where sin abounds, grace must abound more. Because greater is He who is in you, than the one, who is in the world. 1 John 4:4 For we all have sinned and fallen short of the glory of God, being justified freely by His grace through the redemption that is in Christ Jesus whom God set forth as propitiation by His blood, through faith, to demonstrate His righteousness. Romans 3:23-24.

It was the last Monday in the month of January 2014. I was 35. It was like any other day. I was excited about some really nice fabric from my mom to sew a dress.

"Look Nova! This is for us to make matching outfits!" Nova was looking at me. She rarely ever took her Bambi-brown eyes off of me. Yes, I had picked the perfect dog. I was planning to make Nova a matching scarf so that the scarves would complement one another when we went for walks together. I had drugs to smoke, so everything was going well.

Tyler and Jay came over. We made Jell-O, plus I baked a cake. Jay helped me bake the cake. It was one of those rainbow flavour ones, and the batter always tasted so good. We baked it up, and by the time the Jell-O had set, everything was done.

Jay was playing his guitar when Tyler suggested, "Hey should we go get some dope. I think Shew is home."

Jay looked up from his guitar, "Sure, lets go."

"I will go with my own car and meet you guys there."

"Okay, see you there."

They left and I shut the door. The breeze of winter cold came in. I turned around and went down to my room. I stood in front of my dresser.

Everything from this moment on changed in my life.

EIGHTEEN
BORN AGAIN

God allowed me right then to have a glimpse of what was waiting for me on the other side of my choices. Cast down and delivered into chains of darkness. 2 Peter 2:4 Evil swarmed all around me in the room. *"Sinner! Death by fire!"* It was the evil that condemned me. I had never understood anything like this before. I could see and feel the spiritual realm. I was standing in two different rooms. One in this world and one in the next. I felt what God holds back. I saw God's mercy on our souls and what He is protecting us from. Evil beyond human comprehension.

I was in a small holding cell. Solitary confinement, except for the evil creatures swarming me, lunging at me, wanting to devour me. They had me surrounded. I was trapped and paralyzed in fear. I looked to my left, feeling murderous hatred and wanting desperately to escape. I looked away, and up to God, searching for where He was in all of this.

I cried out, "No! I'm not meant to go here!"

WHY DO THE WICKED RENOUNCE GOD? HE HAS SAID IN HIS HEART, YOU WILL NOT REQUIRE AN ACCOUNT. Psalm 10:13.

Hell is a place of unspeakable pain, unimaginable horror, and unthinkable evil. Unrelenting torment and eternal damnation. There are no words I can use to express the reality of this evil. There will be no letting up. The intensity of fear surpasses a human capacity that is measurable.

I kept looking up, looking to God, to see what was going on.

Death is what they call the great equalizer, where everything that is wrong will be made right and where justice is served. The fear you have run from your entire life will be by your side, haunting you evermore. There are no more second chances, not a chance to beg or plead for mercy. You are there for a reason, and you are there eternity.

God opened my understanding that I might comprehend. Luke 24:45

I looked around my room. Above me, a heavy curtain opened up. Suddenly, I was standing in a Throne Room. I was in the presence of God.

There was no one else to blame for any of my choices. There was no time. I was fully responsible for every choice I had ever made. Just Him and I. Everything was clear. God stopped the world for me in this exact moment. I was speechless. I stood still. Waiting to hear what God was going to say.

God spoke, saying this: "THIS IS WHAT YOU CHOSE."

For the first time, I had holy, reverent fear of God. I was expecting the wrath of God. I was ready to see His anger and for God to throw all my mistakes in my face, but that is not what happened. He did not accuse me.

God did not want to destroy me; He wanted to spare me. He was not there to hurt me; He was on my side. God loved me and wanted to show me something that I needed to understand. I had rejected the Son of God, Jesus Christ.

Next, I was shown a vision of Jesus Christ's Crucifixion. It was the back of the cross and the top half. I did not see the front; for God had mercy on my eyes.

> Just as there were many who were appalled at Him His appearance was so disfigured beyond that of any man and His form marred beyond human likeness. Isaiah 52:14

> I can assure you of this. And all flesh shall see the salvation of God. Luke 3:6

The curtain closed.

I remained still and utterly horrified, filled with the fear of God.

For God so loved the world that He gave His only begotten Son, that whosoever believes in Him should not perish but have everlasting life. For God did not send His Son into the world to condemn the world, but that the world through Him might be saved. He who believes in Him is not condemned; but he who does not believe is condemned already, because he has not believed in the name of the only begotten Son of God. And this is the condemnation, that the light has come into the world, and men loved the darkness rather than light, because their deeds were evil. For everyone practising evil hates the light and does not come to the light, lest his deeds should be exposed. But he who does the truth comes to the light, that his deeds may be clearly seen, that they have been done in God." John 3:16-21

God needed the perfect atonement for sin, so God sent His Only Son Jesus to die for all of us. Jesus is our sin's atonement. Jesus is sinless. He is the sacrifice. The perfect, pure white lamb.

The feeling inside me sunk so low. How could I have been so careless to all of what Jesus had done for me? I had rejected the Son of God. I was made aware of His love and sacrifice and that anything I had gone through in my life just couldn't match up; there was no comparison.

The trip to hell continued on. I was dead to Christ.

But she who lives in pleasure is dead while she lives. 1 Timothy 5:6

I felt my soul being sucked out of my body. It was ripped out from behind me, from my very core. It was like my soul had been "unplugged". I heard my soul scream out in a demonic voice that I did not recognize. The voice was sick, twisted, screeched out in pain, *"Maria, you're killing yourself!"*

The torment is nothing I wish on anyone. In fact, I'm writing this book to Exalt God, to tell the truth and warn others. I beg you. Hand your life over to Jesus Christ.

I could not afford one more mistake or I would blow it. I could never use, ever again. This was it. I stood in the middle of my bedroom in complete astonishment. I had not measured all the consequences of all my choices, but God had. God had just warned me in full force what would happen to me if I did not change. I can promise you, there is no sin worth committing that is worth even risking going to hell over.

I was still standing still, not going anywhere. I did not know what to do, and I asked, "Okay... what is next? What do I do? Where do I go from here?" I stood and waited, trying to process everything that had just happened. Only God could help me.

Maybe it was a half hour later. When I looked up, I had another vision. It was Jesus Christ. He was wearing white. There was a mountain behind Him (on His right side). It was flat on top, and the colour of it was reddish brown, and there was the sea to His left.

This scripture deeply resonated with what I saw. By way of the sea, beyond the Jordan, in Galilee of the Gentiles. The people who walked in darkness have seen a *great* light, those who dwelt in the land of the shadow of death, upon them a light has shined... For unto us a Child is born, unto us a Son is given; and the government shall be upon His shoulder. And His name will be called Wonderful, Councillor, Mighty God, Everlasting Father, Prince of Peace. The Zeal of the Lord of hosts will preform this. Isaiah 9

I was in awe. I marvelled. Hallelujah! Me, a worthless sinner saw the King of Kings. His Majesty shined on me.
My Savior, Jesus Christ, spoke to me and said.

"YOU ARE NOT ALONE. I WILL GET YOU
THROUGH THIS. IF YOU FOLLOW ME."
THEN, HE OFFERED ME HIS HAND.

I was astonished. In love. Speechless with Joy.
Most undeserving. I was confronted with clarity.
Jesus was wounded! But yet, my sins were freely forgiven.
The chains could not hold against the authority of The Lord!
I knew Him by His love. I was humbled by His
grace. And the Truth set me free!
"PRICE PAID"
A gift of mercy from His Most Excellency.

For this is what The Lord says; "You were sold for nothing, and without money you will be redeemed." Isaiah 52:3

In that moment, I finally understood where I was. I saw that I was standing in the outer blackness.

> But the sons of the kingdom will be cast out into outer darkness. There will be weeping and gnashing of teeth. Matthew 8:12

I gave Jesus Christ my hand and He took it. I let Him pull me up. I was smiling at Jesus, the Christ of God! He pulled me up out of the pit and stood me on the solid rock. I was rescued! Thank You Jesus Christ! Praise the Lord! Are there words I can use to express this? Humbled. Thank You Lord.

I was up for a few more hours that night, in shock. I was reeling in the intensity of an experience that had left me in a world neither here nor there, but somewhere in between that I was still coming back from.

It is clear. Anyone can be forgiven of their sins. Repent (confess) your sins and turn from them. Chose not sin. Cleave to Jesus Christ. Repentance is a great thing. It takes the weight of your sins and pulls it out of your heart. It sets you free! If you want to be free, go to Jesus Christ! This is how you start developing a trusting relationship with God. By being honest. Jesus said, "But unless you repent, you too will all perish." Luke 13:5

I woke up the next day at 6:45 p.m. I needed to get to a recovery meeting. I needed to talk to Rita. I needed to get to that Life Church. I knew the meeting started at 7 p.m. I did not care what condition I was in and walked in dishevelled. The Holy Spirit guided me.

At the end of the evening, I was using the washroom.

Rita came in and asked, "Is there anything I can do for you?" she said. Her eyes were caring and soft.

I looked at her, dead serious, and said, "Pray like my life depends on it."

So right there in the washroom, Rita did not hesitate. She grabbed my hands in hers. We stood there, with hands locked, heads bowed, and eyes closed. Rita began to pray out loud. She summoned Thee Most High God. Instantly the power was upon me. Rita prayed for my complete deliverance. She prayed for a complete restoration of my mind, body, and soul. I repeated after Rita and re-gave my soul over to the Lord.

As I stood there, I felt the wind begin blowing into my soul. It was alive and travelling steady! The Holy Spirit began filling my entire body. Just the night before, where I had felt my dead soul being sucked out; now, breath was being breathed back through it. The Holy Spirit blew, and blew, and blew. It was filling my entire body. I was awestruck. A moment later, I heard the water start to come trickling in. I was blown away. It was an intricate stream. Gentle living waters were flowing into me, coming from my belly. It sounded calm – gagosh, gagosh, gagosh, gagosh, gagosh. I was still. I wanted it to keep filling me. I welcomed it so. Each second, a force so incredibly powerful was bringing me back to life. I allowed the Holy Spirit to fill me to the point I was overflowing with breath. The Holy Spirit wanted to be in all of me, into my very pores. I felt the pressure in my chest being pushed out, like a balloon that was going to burst. I needed to exhale. I started to breathe again. It felt like I hadn't for years. I had been dead and was being brought back to life. When the Holy Spirit was finished doing its work inside of me, I lifted my head and opened my eyes. I was revived.

"If anyone thirsts, let him come to Me and drink. He who believes in Me, as the Scripture has said, out of his belly will flow rivers of living water." John 7:37

I was born again. So, what does the New Birth mean?

Jesus said, "Most assuredly, I say to you, unless one is born again, he cannot see the kingdom of God." The wind blows where it wishes, and you hear the sound of it, but cannot tell where it comes from and where it goes. So is everyone who is born of the Spirit. John 3:3,7

> The new birth, or regeneration (Titus 3:5), is the act by which God imparts spiritual life to one who trusts in Christ. Without this spiritual birth, a person cannot perceive spiritual things, nor can they enter the Kingdom of God.

I felt the difference between being dead and now being alive. I felt incredible! I was born again! I knew in that moment I would absolutely make it! I was literally transformed. It was the unstoppable force of The Holy Spirit.

I walked home that night, knowing my chains were gone. The enemy was majorly defeated. I understood the magnitude of what Jesus Christ did for me, the significant implications. If what just happened to me broke my addiction, and filled me with power; then what about the other addicts? What would happen if people repented of their sins and trusted in Jesus Christ? When people decided enough is enough, surrendered, and completely turned to Jesus for *complete deliverance.* I know the truth, and the truth set me completely free.

I strolled along. I had been released. Down the sidewalk I went with my head held high, savouring every second of this newness of life. I was alive again! As we walked, the Holy Spirit said to me, "You are only just one piece of something so much greater than you could ever imagine."

I am in complete awe of God. In a world of uncertainty, there is only one truth: Jesus Christ.

This is He who came by water and blood – Jesus Christ; not
only by water, but by water and blood. And it is the Spirit
who bears witness, because the Spirit is truth. For there are
three that bear witness in heaven: The Father, the Word, and
the Holy Spirit, and these three are one. 1 John 5:6-8.

Within twenty-four hours, I heard from God, my Father in heaven.
I met my Savior, Jesus Christ. I was filled with the Holy Spirit.
Indeed, the trinity. The three were individual but acting as one. Praise
Jesus. Hallelujah!

I immediately started attending church. It was essential I be joined to
the body of Christ. That is what the church is. It offers vital spiritual
protection. I took a back seat on the church bench pew and brought
my vulnerability. I had to be obedient and come back home to the
heart of Jesus Christ, His bride, the church. The Sunday topic: "Love
your neighbour." If anyone needed love, it was me. If anyone needed to
learn how to love others, that was me too.

The days passed. I was steady filled with the Holy Spirit. I did not
understand why I felt so good. The Holy Spirit empowered me over
the addiction. I was enthusiastic about life! This was new life and I was
fully alive! I spent part of my time with Dallas, her husband and kids.
Every day of the week, for a week, Dallas had a gift waiting for me on
her table, encouraging my recovery. I am indebted to my entire family
for all their help.

The months passed. I lived in the word of God. As I searched through
my Bible, God spoke to me clearly, giving me my last warning:

"COME NOW, AND LET US REASON TOGETHER. THOUGH YOUR SINS ARE LIKE SCARLET, THEY SHALL BE WHITE AS SNOW; THOUGH THEY ARE RED LIKE CRIMSON, THEY SHALL BE AS WOOL. IF YOU ARE WILLING AND OBEDIENT, YOU SHALL EAT THE GOOD OF THE LAND; BUT IF YOU REFUSE AND REBEL, YOU SHALL BE DEVOURED BY THE SWORD, FOR THE MOUTH OF THE LORD HAS SPOKEN." Isaiah 1:19

His words were final. If I was to fall, it would be forever, cast into the dark kingdom and away from His goodness. Forever.

"I understand Father. Thank you."

NINETEEN

SHIELD OF FAITH

Three years later, I wake up feeling brand-new! God is good beyond measure. I know Jesus is right there, by my side. Listening to the band Third Day, I'm on my knees and the melody rings, "God, I'm running for Your heart until I am a soul on fire..." The song literally ignites the sparks within my heart. I close my eyes. I see the smoke begin to rise up. This is worship – I'm moved!

The passion I found, His name is the Lord Jesus Christ. Do you know Him? I want the Holy Spirit to consume me! I delight in Him and feel exceedingly glad. I want more. Can one ever get enough of Him once they have felt and depended on His goodness? I want to be more consumed by the Mighty God more today than I was yesterday. When I praise His name, I feel my heart leaping within me. I'm certain He is there abiding in me and I in Him.

It was like change tables being overturned. One encounter with Jesus Christ flipped my world back over instantly. I love Jesus with all my heart. I love Him, I love Him, I love Him! My days may be a bit up and down, but He is steady. In the midst of life's problems and pain, I'm constantly comforted by the Prince of Peace. He is the only one I can trust. I have to keep my focus on Him. I follow Him.

We have travelled over the wild stormy seas and made it through the night. I was curled up in the bow of a humble boat, frightened beyond comprehension. We kept going. Jesus Christ rowed the boat safely across to the other side. And He leads and He leads. We walk through the sands, down the slopes, and at the foot of the mountain we stopped to pray. So where are we going? I know He is taking me somewhere very special, and it turned into a love story.

Life is not easy. As time passed, I started feeling volcanoes erupting in my life. Trying to figure out who I'm supposed to be and where I'm supposed to go has been a struggle because I was clueless to the simplicity of the hardness of life. In a heart beat, I gave up every "friend" I had used drugs with and started on an entirely incredible new journey.

We went the long way around. I know that God loves me and He will never fail me. That is a huge comfort. I had a mind with uncertainty, this is from the enemy. Jesus showed me that when no one else would be there for me, He always would be. I have walked with Him. This is how I know He is Faithful and True. He never let me down. In the darkness He is there, I learned to call out to Him. Walking in the Spirit. Trusting and believing in God. I gave Him control and surrendered to Him.

I had a tough time understanding how come God was not mad at me. When God pulled the curtain back in my room, I was expecting the wrath of God. It finally clicked. Jesus Christ took the wrath of God for me. I should have suffered. But Jesus suffered for me.

Sitting in church, the young man spoke, "If you are angry at God, He can handle your anger. It will not change the fact that He loves you. Things are not always all good. Sometimes we have secrets. But God already knows. Just get the lies out."

I could not agree more. God loves you! God is the source of life! He has everything we need. He has the wisdom. Leave your past at the cross. Surrender, and let your healing begin.

Dear Father, I ask for heavenly wisdom to help others. I desperately need You. Please Jesus, be my first love forever. Thank You for Your fruit, flowers, and the showers of blessings. May Your Holy Word dwell richly in my soul. Wash my soul Lord, please. Fix all the broken in me. Only You can. I love Your righteousness and all that You are. Thank you for setting me free. I'm Your child. In Jesus Christ. Amen.

> I in them, and You in Me, that they may be made perfect in one, and that the world may know that You have sent Me, and have loved them as You have loved Me. John 17:23

> Sanctify us by Your truth. Your word is truth. John 17:17

And now I know I was made just for Him. And now I know I was made to adore Him.

God is the lover of my soul. When fear comes. I am in awe. How much greater You are.
It is Your Presence that overwhelms me. There is none like You.
I asked You, "What do You see when You look at me?"
Your one word pierced my heart deeply.
It was sharper than any blade that cut.
"Love"
I heard You early morning, when the day light rose.
You called me, "Blessed"
Tears roll down my face. I felt the chains fall off my soul.
You are the one my soul loves.
I praise You Lord. You are the only reason why I stand.

I had sinned against God and heaven, against my own soul.
A worthless sinner that received Your grace.
Down on my knees I found your mercy. And You took me back.
Simply to know of Your goodness changes the wounded heart.

You tear down, root out, and rebuild. Restorer of broken walls.
You water day and night. I grow.
You love me. Thank You for tending my vineyard.

I lay my head on my pillow.
God you are always up to something.
Your love is a treasure hunt. I seek and I find You.
You bloomed a flower in my heart. You slobbered on my cheek.
How real You are.
Surely now my King.
Your healing hands I hold. All I ask is that You take me higher.
There I shall find the fragrant spices. In the aroma of Your intoxicating Love.

We are a people that need to know Your goodness.
That need to not sin against You.
Teach us to worship You in Spirit and in Truth.
Simply because You are awesome.
And on the other side of our doubts.
That is where You reign. Your rule does not change with the tide.
You expect our all.
You still move the mountains to rescue us.
You still heal, and Your miracles are great.
You will break our chains when we humble ourselves to You.
Nothing is to impossible for you.

We need to surrender to a God that loves to give us peace.

Your word is a wonderland of promises that you do not break.
And I'm seeking Your face and press on my knees.
Change our hearts my Gracious Lord.
Let us surrender and turn back to You.
No one can compare. To Your Majesty, kindness and grace.

Your rivers and valleys will turn into peaks all around you.
You are with me for life. Timeless. We always were.

Praise God! Thank You Lord.

Within the first year of my recovery, my parents, Dallas, and the youth
pastor Ted encouraged me to go on a mission trip to Mexico. It would
be about two weeks long. It was with the Baptist church. We would
stay in a compound while we were there, and during the day, we would
build houses for the poor. I immediately shut it down.

"No way." I said after Dallas asked me. Are you kidding? I did not
trust anyone. After twelve solid years of extreme drug use (taking out
all the breaks), I was "diagnosed" with extreme social anxiety, which
is fear of people, and a borderline personality disorder. I'm kind of
intense, not to mention, I'm a recovering crystal meth addict. Hello?
I have a serious malfunction in the junction. I need healing. Yes, I was
free from addiction, but a prisoner of fear in my mind. Just the thought
of going was so far out of my comfort zone it was not in the realm
of possibility. Oh, I talked of Jesus and how I loved Jesus so, but to
head off to Mexico was a bit extreme. This was unsafe for me. I would
have no where to hide. I mean, I could talk the talk, but could I walk
the walk?

"No." I rationalized my decision. I could not leave my two beautiful
dogs, Nova and Scarlet. I was convinced that I would end up having
problems with everyone.

Over the next few months, the idea of going to Mexico still was in question. I felt like the Lord actually wanted me to go. Maybe I needed to trust Him, no matter how difficult it would be. So, I dropped all my fears. It truly was tough. I can honestly confess I was hands down, the worst missionary who was ever born. I was under severe oppression the entire time. I felt alone. I did not understand how to manage my thoughts, or how to chase them away.

To my great shame, and no surprise to me, I lashed out. I was counting down. How long could I hold the pain inside for -before I blew. I was in fights with my sister Dallas, and I'm talking about screaming at her. I snapped at the driver of the vehicle, who was an elder in my church. Plus, I had it out with the youth pastor. I was irritated with almost the whole group. Just because I was off drugs did not mean I did not have major issues to work through. I was completely broken inside. Maybe I was expecting everyone else to fix me. Expecting someone to see my pain. Instead of turning to God and giving it to Him.

I did not get these people, and these people did not get me. These "Christians" were so happy. It seemed I was nothing like them. Did I belong? And the doubting began. I started to think if this was being a Christian, I just could not do it. I was miserable. The trip was not making any sense. Surely following Jesus would be easy? But that was not the case. All I wanted was to build the houses for the poor as quickly as possible; so I could get back to the compound and cross the day off my calendar. Then I would be back home that much quicker.

My heart was softened as I walked down the old dilapidated staircase that belonged to Elizabeth; we were building a home for her. She was a mother of five children. She was tiny.

Her place was on a steep hill. Around us there were millions of other little homes. In one direction you could see rich houses, and the other way lived the poor. The stairs to get down to her shack were steep. The railing was totally unsafe and ready to buckle at any moment.

Over the next few hours, between hammering in nails and taking a break from the scolding hot sun, I watched her four young boys playing. They were truly happy. I felt Elizabeth's sweetness. I got the sense that she was a very strong woman in Jesus, who knew who she was, and I could feel her peace. A simple life with a roof over her head on a cold concrete pad. She was blessed. I thought these people who had virtually nothing were weak, but now I realize, they are the ones who are strong.

When we were leaving at the end of the day, I hugged Elizabeth tightly and held on. With all my heart did I not want to let her go. I kissed her over and over on the cheek. I felt I belonged with them. This was where true love existed. The team packed up the truck, and we were about to leave, when Elizabeth came running after us with two bright-white, cotton, hand-embroidered gifts for my sister and me. Dallas and I were touched how Elizabeth gave out of her little.

Back at the compound, I watched the mission team. How could I justify any of my actions? The anger I had inside I took out on those around me. I was a jerk. I confess that I did not glorify God at all. I was so different from everyone there. I was constantly in my head, thinking nonstop, to the point of confusion. I lay in bed wondering to myself. I was not like other "Christians".

I fell asleep and woke up the next morning feeling a little different. Instead of Dallas serving me coffee, I wanted to bring her coffee. I grabbed my Bible devotional and headed outside to read God's Word. Sitting there, I felt the warmth of a Mexican August. I could feel it was an extra special moment. As I read the devotional, tears started to roll down my cheeks. What an epic fail. I was raw with emotions.

I felt like I had messed up the entire mission trip. The liar and enemy of my soul told me, "I was not worthy to be loved." I had been a horrible and a mean person to others. I had no self control. It broke my heart. These hard emotions were coming at me. Then Jesus gently told me, "No matter how bad you feel about yourself, I will never leave you."

I was still. His peace and comfort were incredible. His words were medicine that soothed my broken soul. The entire time I had not realized that Jesus was with me; by my side faithfully. Jesus' words soothed my fears, doubts, and feelings of worthlessness. He wiped my tears away, and I stopped crying. Another treasured stolen moment. No, He never said it would be easy. But He promised to never leave us.

> And lo, I am with you always, even to the
> end of age. Amen. Matthew 28:20

My perception of life completely changed right there. That morning I found myself. It hit home. After all the years of being lost and blind, I understood. I had just found my identity in Jesus Christ. It took me a journey to find myself in Jesus. I was sure. *He would never leave me.* This verse ministered to me right there:

> He who finds his life will lose it, and he who loses his
> life for My sake will find it. Matthew 10:39

Sometimes life makes us feel so down. Things will get better, just go to The Lord. It was in my pain where I found Him. His voice can be heard when we are still. I am learning that He is what life is all about. You need to realize too, that if you are hurting, God is right there by your side. The moment we turn to Him, He is listening and He is our helper.

When I got back home from Mexico, I started writing this book. My parents encouraged me to share it. God boosted me up and gave me the confidence.

I also had to start employment.

After my first eight-hour shift, I walked into my bedroom and sat on my bed, totally exhausted. I lay back on my pillow. Not having a clue. I was headed into a category 9 storm.

A legion of demons waited for me. Ready to tackle me in an onslaught. I had no clue why, nor did I see it coming.

No one likes you, Joy. You are alone! Your sister hates you. Your parents can't handle you. You're nothing! Your other sister does not like you either. You are totally alone!

The problem with what they were saying was that I believed them, and it was kind of true.

What! You can't work this job! You can't do it!

Demon after demon was coming after my mind. I felt myself shrinking inside, considering what they were forcibly yelling at me. The principalities of darkness shrouded me in thick torment. I began sobbing in mental and emotional derailment.

You're alone in this one, the evil lied.

It told me one lie after another. It wanted to control me, hold me down with it, to make me sink a little lower and make me feel ever more less. Twenty minutes passed, an hour passed, I felt paralyzed.

The Bible once again gives light to the situation, explaining:

FINALLY, MY BRETHREN, BE STRONG IN THE LORD AND IN THE POWER OF HIS MIGHT. PUT ON THE WHOLE ARMOUR OF GOD, THAT YOU MAY BE ABLE TO STAND AGAINST THE WILES OF THE DEVIL. FOR WE DO NOT WRESTLE AGAINST FLESH AND BLOOD, BUT AGAINST PRINCIPALITIES, AGAINST POWERS, AGAINST THE RULERS OF THE DARKNESS OF THIS AGE, AGAINST SPIRITUAL HOSTS OF WICKEDNESS IN THE HEAVENLY PLACES. THEREFORE, TAKE UP THE WHOLE ARMOUR OF GOD, THAT YOU MAY BE ABLE TO WITHSTAND IN THE EVIL DAY, AND HAVING DONE ALL, TO STAND. STAND THEREFORE, HAVING GIRDED

YOUR WAIST WITH TRUTH, HAVING PUT ON THE BREASTPLATE
OF RIGHTEOUSNESS, AND HAVING SHOD YOUR FEET WITH
PREPARATION OF THE GOSPEL OF PEACE; ABOVE ALL, TAKING
THE SHIELD OF FAITH WITH WHICH YOU WILL BE ABLE TO
QUENCH ALL THE FIERY DARTS OF THE WICKED ONE. AND
TAKE THE HELMET OF SALVATION, AND THE SWORD OF THE
SPIRIT, WHICH IS THE WORD OF GOD. EPHESIANS 6:10-17

You're crazy! You need to go to a mental hospital, not get a job! You can't hold down a job! You
   have lost your mind!

And somehow, for a moment, I literally lost my mind. I did not know who I was. I did not know how I could defend myself. I did not know anything, except the evil that attacked me. Then my mind swooped back to me. It was the second scariest feeling I had ever felt.

"Why is this happening?" I agonized aloud.

"Why won't this stop?"

I trusted God's goodness and mercy, even under the constant trauma of this. Where was God? I was looking to Him in this darkness.

To my amazement, I suddenly understood what exactly was happening to me – it was the fiery darts of the wicked one. They were hitting my head and attacking me over and over with intentions to destroy me. All the drugs I had used over my life time to deal with the pain, abuse, and to avoid feeling anything, turned against me, coming at me with full force. No matter how hard I had tried to avoid my feelings, they had never gone away.

In the mist of everything, I had another moment of clarity. I had been reading from my grandma's Bible, in the book of Psalms. I remembered King David asked God, "Search my heart." That moment was speaking strongly. I knew that Jesus was in my heart. All I could do was ask Him.

Through my tears, I managed to muster up enough courage, "Are these thoughts attacking me true?" I took hold of the thought to ask my heart. Before it came near to my heart, it ricocheted off. I heard a loud "clank," it deflected off the metal armour that was around my heart. It struck me astounded.

I started taking the rest of the lies and sent them to ask my heart. Each fiery dart bounced off. I began to have more clarity in my mind from the protection of the shield. I positioned myself and hid behind the shield to get cover.

One after the other, I felt God's protection, truth, and the power. My mind for the first time was safe. My strength began to return to me. It was incredible for me to win. To know the power of God is there to protect us all from the enemy. I was ready to declare the victory, and I yelled out loud, "In the name of Jesus Christ, I bind you evil, GO to hell!" And it was finished.

TWENTY

PRAISE GOD!

"Fear not, for I am with you; be not dismayed, for I am
your God. I will strengthen you, yes, I will help you, I will
uphold you with My righteous right hand." Isaiah 41:10

After my first year of recovery I stood in the hallway of my trailer,
when the Holy Spirit told me, "I will get you through the next year." I
was startled. I will never know in this life the full extent of how God
protected my life from harm.

On the second year of recovery the Holy Spirit spoke to me again,
"I will get you through your next year." Jesus was Faithful and got
me through.

He told me, "Let us work on Your restoration." How great is God!

Another nice surprise; Cassie quit using drugs too at the same time.
She got victory! Praise the Lord!

My dear friend Rita has a heart for the broken. She suggested to
me, "Make goals for yourself." This is a powerful tool if you tend to get
stuck. Hopefully, we have those days when we wake up and want more
out of life.

My sister Remi would lovingly say to me, "Be kind to yourself." You are who The Lord says you are.

It is my choice how I handle problems. It is tough not having a "crutch". Truth be told, having a crutch slowed me down. It left me behind.

Remember the lamb of God. He did not say a word. Jesus was led as a sheep to the slaughter; and as a lamb before its shearer is silent, so He opened not His mouth. In His humiliation His justice was taken away, and who will declare His generation? For His life was taken from the earth. Acts 8:32 Scripture demonstrated His peace and the sovereign power of God. God is in complete control of the entire situation.

Recovery is day by day. I am not smart. I know nothing and I have struggled. But Jesus Christ knows all. God let me know my underlying issues. I need major inner healing. This is a journey of time and restoration within my soul. Fear and pride controlled my choices and my emotions. They consumed me. It tied me up and destroyed me every way it could. Thankfully, God is bigger than any problem I will ever have.

Jesus Christ has not given us a spirit of fear, but of love, power, and a sound mind. 2 Timothy 1:7

I had to learn that any negative feeling is a lie. I had to take charge. I learn to command those feelings, "Go Away!" And they listen. This is incredible truth. Jesus Christ is the truth. Jesus Christ is the light! Declare light and you will win any battle. I learn to replace the lies with the Word of God. When the forceful emotion tells me, "I am alone," now I tell it, "That is a lie. Jesus Christ is right here. Get lost. In Jesus name." This is a process and takes consistency. Praise God.

Repairer of broken walls. Isaiah 58:12

I beseech you therefore, brethren, by the mercies of God, that
you present your bodies a living sacrifice, holy, acceptable
to God, which is your reasonable service. And do not be
conformed to the world, but be transformed by the renewing
of your mind, that you may prove what is that good and
acceptable and perfect will of God. Romans 12:1,2

If my relationship is right with God, it will not matter what others
think. All that matters is what God thinks. Maybe deep down I
thought I would fail God. But the thing is, God will never fail me. It
is never going to be my strength; it is going to be God's strength. If I
could do it on my own, then where would that leave Jesus? Jesus Christ
is our deliver. Surrendering is the best decision I ever made!

I still am climbing mountains. Praise God for the place where sweet
nectar flows. Drink from the well inside; the source of life. I live in
peace and follow Jesus. So much I learn along the way! I am jubilant! I
have many songs of joy and praise to sing as I go. On the other side of
the lies we tend to hold onto and believe, is our Promised Land. Jesus
Christ is trying to lead us into a state of constant peace, despite any
circumstance. The enemy does not want us to find this kingdom. He
deceives us, keeps us distracted by our problems, and with incredibly
less things.

The worldly things we have trouble giving up are the things we need
to let go of. On the other side is complete freedom and the tranquility
of peace. The world is in one direction and the promised land is in the
other. So how do you get into this kingdom? Follow Jesus Christ.

Seek ye first the kingdom of God and its righteousness. Matthew 6:33

Jesus Christ said, "the kingdom of God is within you" Luke 17:21

Life is but a matter of the condition of the heart. Just when I think I have confessed all my sin, shared my struggles and hopes, we come to the next layer of the heart. I realize wow, I have not even scratched the surface; then He shows me more. How intimate. My desire is to find out more of who this amazing God is. What He has shown me is that He is great. We share this journey together. What an amazing patient God. It makes me stand in awe. He takes me inside myself. He searches the depths with me. It makes me want to keep going, seeking, following. Time with God there is always going to be more to discover. Who can fathom this gentle trust? This all-knowing God. God is the guard of my soul. He is faithfully dedicated to my perfection to maturity and success to be free in Him. His mercy constantly holds. And what does He do with my confessions? He removes them as far as the east is from the west. Psalm 103:12

You got relationship problems? Write them down to God and talk to Him. Whatever issues you got, write them down. Address it God and pray about. When you seek Him, you will find Him. He will answer. He is the best husband and Father you could get.

After I wrote the last paragraph, I stopped for the night. I bathed and went to my room to read my Bible and talk with God. I felt astoundingly good. I shut off my lights, ready to fall asleep. I felt amazing, incredible deep peace. It is something so special. I love the feeling of being very near to God. As I lay there, the anchor of love appeared. And we connected. Lord, what is all waiting on the other side, past the torn veil? Grab hold of the anchor and learn how to breathe the water. There we experience intimacy and hear the language of God.

"Continue in the faith and saying that through many tribulations we enter the kingdom of God." The Acts of The Apostles. 14:22.

The gospel message may be simple, but it is not easy. Sin is a choice. There are two trees we can choose to eat from. The tree of life, or the forbidden fruit. I heard from a missionary once, "Sin does not actually exist until we do it."

And it shall come to pass in the last days, says God, that I will pour out My Spirit on all flesh; your sons and your daughters shall prophesy; your young men shall see visions, your old men shall dream dreams. I will show wonder in heaven above and signs in the earth beneath. The Acts of the Apostles 2:17

"I, the Lord, have called you in righteousness, and will hold your hand; I will keep you and give you as a covenant to the people, as a light to the Gentiles, to open blind eyes, to bring out prisoners from the prison, those who sit in darkness from the prison house. I am the Lord, that is My name; and my glory I will not give to another, nor my praise to carved images. Behold, the former things have come to pass, and new things I declare; Before they spring forth I tell you of them." Isaiah 42:7-9

Through the Lord's mercies we are not consumed, because His compassion's fail not, they are new every morning; great is Your Faithfulness. "The Lord is my portion," says my soul, therefore I hope in Him. Lamentations 3:22

Listen, who have been upheld by Me from birth, who have been carried from the womb: Even to your old age I am He, and even to grey hairs, I will carry you! I have made, and I will bear; even I will carry, and will deliver you. To whom will you liken Me, and make Me equal and compare Me, that we should be alike. Isaiah 46:3-5

As the heavens are higher than the earth, so are My way higher
than your ways and My thoughts than your thoughts. Isaiah 55:9

"And new things I declare; before they spring
forth I tell you of them." Isaiah 42:9
God is amazing. There is no other God that declares, "I will restore."

Therefore, if anyone is in Christ, he is a new creation;
old things have passed away; behold, all things
have become new. 2 Corinthians 5:17

I know whatever God does, it shall be forever.
Nothing can be added to it, and nothing taken from it.
God does it, that men should fear before Him.
That which is has already been.
And what is to be has already been;
And God requires an account of what is past.
Ecclesiastes 3: 14,15

Then He who sat on the throne said, "Behold, I make
all things new." And He said to me, "Write, for these
words are true and faithful." Revelations 21:5

I love you Jesus. Thank You.

TWENTY-ONE
ONLY ONE WAY

Salvation is found in no one else, for there is no other name under
heaven given to men by which we must be saved. Acts 4:12

That if you confess with your mouth the Lord is Jesus
and believe in your heart that God has raised Him
from the dead, you will be saved. Romans 10:9

And if it is by grace, then it is no longer of works;
otherwise grace is no longer grace. Romans 11:6

He who believes and is baptized will be saved, but he who
does not believe will be condemned. Mark 16:16

The Lord is not slack concerning His promise, not willing that any
should perish but that *all* should come to repentance. 2 Peter 3:9

Jesus answered, "I am the way and the truth and the light. No one
comes to the Father except through me." John 14:6 Jesus does not just
tell us to figure it out, He says, "I am the way." If you're confused, He
says, "He is the truth." If you are surrendered to the Lordship, this is

great, as He is our All and All. This is exclusive. It is narrow. He says, "Come to me." Jesus says, "I am the gate." There are two gates and there are two roads, but there is only one way to heaven. It is precise; it is narrow. It is more then just heaven one way and hell the other. It is all a spectrum. If Jesus says something is right, then anything that contradicts it is wrong.

"Come to me, all you who are weary and burdened, and I will give you rest. Take my yoke upon you and learn from me, for I am gentle and humble in heart, and you will find rest for your souls. For my yoke is easy and my burden is light." Matthew 11:2-30

Do not be afraid; I Am the First and the Last. I Am He who lives, and was dead, and behold, I Am alive forevermore. Amen. And I have the keys of Hades and of Death. Revelation 1:18

Dear Reader:

God loves you and I love you. I pray that you will consider opening your heart up to God. Everyone is welcome to receive God's grace, a new life, and the gift of salvation. When you finish reading, I encourage you to take time to look within yourself. My hope is that you get your heart right before God. If you desire God to change your world, then get on your knees and face God in this life, so that you are prepared for the next. Go into His Throne Room today. Into His very presence. Repent your sins so that you may receive forgiveness. Plant the seed of faith in your heart. Nurture and protect it. Accept Jesus Christ as your Lord and Saviour. Surrender to His Lordship daily. Ask Him to change your heart and to break all your chains. He will. And let your incredible journey begin.

"Lord Heavenly Father:

I come into Your Presence Lord. I give You all my Praise. I pray for those who need freedom, I pray for people who need Your Salvation. May they choose to receive it. I ask You release Your Holy Spirit to us.

Your Mighty right arm is outstretched; it is held out for any one who wants to grab hold of it. You are ready to deliver and lift people up out of the pit when they call on You.

Prince of Peace. Revive souls that are dead. Call Your wayward children home. Holy Spirit, overflow our cups! Please Lord, bring a complete healing and restoration into mind, spirit, body, and soul.

I ask in Jesus Christ name. Amen.

Thank you Lord. I praise You."

TWENTY-TWO

FELLOWSHIP

God shows me where I stand with Him; I feel Your warmth within me. You want me to know of your goodness and mercy. These are things you do not want to withhold.

The mistakes of my past, I have been forgiven. The one thing you desire is my heart.

How pure of a love to consider the most inner ward parts within me. You measure soul, heart, and the corridors within us.

You know exactly how much room within needs to be changed, filled, and renewed.

Your words are the constant truth.

Four years into my recovery, I heard the still, small voice again. "We miss having fellowship with you. Rise early tomorrow. Fellowship with us."

I answered, "Okay, I will."

The next morning, I was woken up early by the Holy Spirit. It was still dark outside. I grabbed my Bible and started reading. I got to a parable that was speaking strongly to me, so I focused all my attention on it. What was it trying to tell me? It was the book of Mathew. Jesus takes a blind man by the hand, leads him into the wilderness, and restores his sight. I read it over many times, thinking on and appreciating it. I shut my eyes to pray, and right in front of me was a bright white, small light. I was in awe of the glory of God.

That which we have seen and heard we declare unto you, that ye also may have fellowship with us: and truly our fellowship is with the Father, and with His Son Jesus Christ. And these things write we unto you, that your joy may be full. This then is the message which we have heard of Him, and declare unto you, that God is light, and in Him is no darkness at all. 1 John 1: 3-5

A week later, my mom asked me if I wanted to go to the Christian Wilderness Ministries Bible Camp. I thought it was a sign, so I agreed to go. This camp started over twenty years ago. My Aunt and Uncle felt God calling them to start this special ministry. They had ten dollars in the bank. And that is how it all began.

The first night I enjoyed listening to the passionate Dario Martini, a speaker who had come all the way from Brazil. He was a complete stranger, and he is a major part of the revival that is spreading around other parts of the world.

"I preach to all sorts of people, all over the world. We have started treatment centres for these drug addicts," he pronounced with a thick Brazilian accent. Then he boldly declared, "You preach to the worst, you get the best! You preach to the people on drugs, the prostitutes, you get the best! It's true." A chill ran over my body. His words were powerful. They spoke of life and purpose; and they give extraordinary meaning to people hooked on drugs.

"Come to the front. I want to pray for you. Come. Just come."

I got up and walked to the front. I was a little hesitant and completely nervous. I also was excited, not knowing what was going to happen. By now, there was a long line of people standing across up at the front. He came to me first. He took me by the hand. I was freaking out inside, nervous. He placed his hands on me, and my aunt was standing behind me.

"Have you heard the Holy Spirit calling you?" he asked me. I was stunned.

"Yes," I said, nodding definitely.

Then Dario asked, "Have you felt Jesus touching you? Has He touched you? Have you felt Jesus touching you?" *Woe,* I thought, speechless at the thought that Jesus had been touching me.

Dario kept repeating himself, asking me. What? Wow. I did not know what to say. Can I get a witness? Amen. God is good. Yes, I think God has slightly been touching me. God please keep touching me because I love it and I love you. Please Lord Jesus, fill my heart to overflow with rivers of abundant love and faithfulness for Your glory. In Jesus name I ask. Amen.

The third night, I sat up near the front, on the left-hand side. After the singing, the room sat still, worshipping God. Two rows behind me, a lady stood up impromptu and started speaking. She herself was shaky. Her voice was breathy and sounded heavenly. Her lips were anointed and she talked from the Spirit.

"You are my temple.
You are my holy, holy temple.
You must praise me.
For my praise abides in your temple.
You are the vessel of the Lord!
You are the vessel of the Lord!
You are mine!
My chosen people.
For the day that I will return.
I will come and get you!
You are my bride.
I love you.

You must be pure.
Without spot or wrinkle.
How to become pure?
You become pure by my word.
Read my word.
Let it fill your inside being.
May it pour out of your mouth.
May it be abiding in you constantly.
May you think about me.
May you meditate on your pillow.
May you think of the praises of the Lord!
The glory of the Lord!
What I have done for you.
What I have done in your life!
Your praise.
Your praise.
Shall continually be in your mouth.
Hallelujah.
Hallelujah Jesus!
We praise you Lord. Amen."

Praise God! The room was still from the exclamation. Woe is me Lord. I am undone. Those were words of breath and passion. They ministered to the soul and cut the heart. Never should we let go of that dear instruction.

The fourth night I shared my testimony. I did the best I could. At the end of the night, us dear saints were still singing and worshipping. But the enemy was nattering at me, trying to distract me from having my breakthrough. I ignored it and focused on praising God and thanking Him. Then something started happening. The best way I can describe it was that I felt the kingdom gates opened up inside of my chest. I felt *completely forgiven*. From past and future. *It was paid for.*

Jesus paid for every one of my sins. *It is finished.* It was as if I was sitting outside the city gate called Beautiful. More tears of joy and healing for me. I am so blessed. Thank you, God!

The next evening in worship, a lady stood up and declared. "Last night my chains were broken! The Holy Spirit took my smoking addiction from me!" Praise God! The room gave shouts of cheer and a round of applause. Praise God and the power of the Holy Spirit! At the end of the service, we stood at the front. The lady turned to me and gave me a beautiful heart, pearl necklace. She took it right off her neck. Her heart was changed. And that is what it is all about.

> "And now, why are you waiting? Arise and be
> baptized, and wash away your sins, calling on the
> name of the Lord." Acts of The Apostles 22:16

On the second last day of camp, I made the decision to get re-baptized in Tobin Lake. The evening service followed right after, and we gathered under the huge white tent.

We were singing this beautiful hymn: "He is here, hallelujah, He is here, amen, He is here, holy, holy. I will bless His name again. He is here. Listen closely, hear Him calling out your name. He is here, you can touch Him. You will never be the same."

There was a tear in the corner of my eye, and I was standing at the very back. The music dropped off, the room was still. The atmosphere was filled with the Spirit. We were in complete adoration of our Most High God. The Holy Spirit was stirring. Around the room, lingering praises of delicate hallelujah s were lifted up by a few precious saints, and then, it came to me. I heard it in my ears and felt Him writing. His hand was upon me. One word was scribbled across my heart, on the inside. God wrote a new name on my heart. He touched me. And I will never be the same.

Then Jesus said to the twelve, "Do you also want to go away?" But Simon Peter answered Him, "Lord, to whom shall we go? You have the words of eternal life. Also, we have come to believe and know that You are the Christ, the Son of the living God." John 6:68

EPILOGUE

The Holy Spirit put this on my heart. Most of us have seen the movie 'The Titanic.' When the ship goes under, it is a horrific scene. It was the blackest of nights and the water was frigid. Terrified people sat by in life boats waiting to be rescued; while all around them people were drowning. They had eyes, but they could not see the desperation all around them. They had ears but could not hear the screaming cries for help. There hearts were callous. They were spiritually blind. One light cut through the darkness, looking to rescue others.

The light is what the world desperately needs. We owe it to God to give Him our all. Let us win this world over. Let us go out with love and the freedom of the gospel of Jesus Christ. Lord God, we need Your Holy Spirit. Empower us. Thank you for revival. Thank You for the lives You have touched and will touch. Give us eyes to see, ears to hear, and a heart that understands, so that we turn to You, and be healed. We place are full trust in You. I declare there is complete freedom in Jesus Christ. I ask for the glory of the Father, Son, and Holy Spirit. In Jesus Christ. Amen

CPSIA information can be obtained
at www.ICGtesting.com
Printed in the USA
LVHW09s2224190918
590599LV00001B/28/P